PRAISE FOR *NO TRY! ONLY DO...*

"Few people really understand how to simplify the complex like Andy Bailey. Running a growth company is hard; being an entrepreneur is hard. But in this practical, hands-on guide, Andy reduces much of that complexity to simple ideas and strategies. An absolute must-read for entrepreneurs and their teams."

John Ratliff
CEO, Appletree Answers and Align5

"Andy Bailey is a master coach for sure. But it's the depth of his life experience, his triumphs and tragedies, that all entrepreneurs and leaders can learn from."

Stephen R. Satterwhite
founder/CEO, Entelligence, author of *Above the Line*

"*No Try! Only Do* is a mantra in my office because of Andy Bailey. The word 'try' is truly a three-letter word at DS. Because of him, we have created a culture of *I will,* not *I'll try.*"

Danny Daniel
founding partner/OCEO, Daniel Stark Injury Lawyers

"Yoda, he is not. But Master Coach, he is. Andy combines a great sense of humor, a gift for storytelling, and an ability to share the simple structures that can be used as the wire frame for scaling business. He is a coach's coach and has a gift for growing business. This book, read it you must."

Govindh Jayaraman
portfolio entrepreneur, founder, and best-selling author of *Paper Napkin Wisdom*

"Thanks to Andy, *No Try! Only Do* has become a mantra our firm lives by. Andy Bailey is the rare entrepreneur that lives daily by the very words he uses to lead his team and clients. His blend of concepts and real stories makes this a must-read for anyone who wants to elevate their team's performance, and you will forever hear Andy's voice in the back of your head if you ever utter the word *try!*"

Greg Crabtree
CPA, author of *Simple Numbers, Straight Talk, Big Profits*, CEO of Crabtree Rowe & Berger, PC

"Every leader needs to soak up Andy's unique understanding of alignment and its impact on team health and performance. He takes the idea of 'firing on all cylinders' to light speed."

Bill Biggs
COO, Daniel Stark Law, founder, Biggs & Associates

"Engaging Andy Bailey and his team was one of the single best decisions we made for our technology company. We had *tried* implementing the habits for two years, but after working with Andy, the entire team got on board and there was no more trying, we were executing. On exit, it made a financial difference!"

Sonny Clark
founder/president, Acumen Technology

"One of my favorite Andy Bailey sayings is 'WTF—Where's the focus?' Andy is all about teaching teams to focus and execute. Andy's teachings are powerful, simple to implement, and based in real-life experience. Anyone who wants to achieve more with his or her teams must read Andy's book!"

Barrett Ersek
CEO, Holganix, author of *HBR* X-Factor article

"*No Try! Only Do* is a practical roadmap to the personal and professional growth you have been longing to achieve. Andy Bailey's background as a student, entrepreneur and business owner, and corporate coach has afforded him the experiences to know what to do, what not to do, and the most efficient ways to get there. I would encourage you not only to read but dissect and implement the strategies that Andy has been so gracious to share. As a reader, this book will serve as a working manual that you will add to the top of your list of favorites."

Ben L. Looper
founder/CEO, Southeast Restoration

"Start by reading this book to build a better business and design the life you want. Then spend time with Andy Bailey and listen to the story of his life—one that was designed to teach. Lastly, find a great coach, fasten your seatbelt, and get started."

Brian Brault
Entrepreneurs' Organization Global Chairman 2017–18

"Andy's bottom-line approach to business accountability and life is captured in *No Try! Only Do,* a book that challenges you to answer the question *Why?* to all the moving parts of your business. Like a German shepherd who won't let go of the towel, Andy's book continues in its pursuit until you have arrived at a destination located far from your comfort zone—a place where you begin to embrace the world of *How?* which takes you to *Now what?* and most importantly bids you to *Do.*

Just as in his coaching sessions, Andy's book illustrates the value of asking the tough questions, analyzing the right data, accounting for the outcomes—and then repeating, ever in pursuit of business and personal greatness."

Carla DeLoach, Esq.
L.L.M., principle, DeLoach P.L.

"What makes *No Try! Only Do* a remarkable book is that Andy Bailey has been there and done that. Unlike many business coaches, Andy has been in the trenches. He's built companies from the ground up, and he's even had to go back in and completely rebuild a company that had gone off the rails. This isn't a business theory book. This is a business reality book. Buy it today!"

Joe Calloway
author of *Becoming a Category of One*

"If you have been struggling to get your business off the ground or you feel your company is growing too fast, then you need to read Andy Bailey's book *No Try! Only Do.* My company has been coached by Andy and he showed us how to implement the foundational pieces that every business must have. Working with Petra Coach, we grew profits 5x in only three years by utilizing these principles. Read *No Try! Only Do* to learn the must-have principles required in every business."

Corey Cormier
CEO, Legal Monkeys

"I get to work with many entrepreneurs who are extremely bright and have compelling ideas. However, at the end of the day, what distinguishes successful entrepreneurs is the ability to build a team that can execute on a consistent basis. Andy Bailey has helped many businesses, including mine, with development and implementation of the Rockefeller Habits, which provides a roadmap for successful execution. Read this book if you are looking to take your business or organization to a new level."

Charlie Brock
CEO, Launch TN

"Andy Bailey is a concise storyteller, keen listener, and gap savant. The misaligned, ineffective, and unproductive processes, people, and purposes clang like an alarm in his brain. He is the embodiment of the Polish proverb 'A guest sees in an hour what a host misses for a year.' *No Try! Only Do* is a brilliant peek at the journey of service to clients, to causes, to the process of becoming."

Robert Wagnon
friend, dad, CEO

"*No Try! Only Do* is the culmination of the personal and professional experiences of my dear friend Andy Bailey. Having known Andy for over a decade, I have seen him overcome numerous incredible obstacles while achieving the goals he has set out for himself (including building and selling an amazing company). Those who Andy has coached have seen similar results."

Ken Sim
BOG Brother, CEO of Nurse Next Door and Rosemary Rocksalt

"*No Try! Only Do* has been Andy Bailey's mantra for the decade-plus I've known him. His straight-forward, no-nonsense approach to getting things done has not only allowed him to build the nation's most successful coaching firm, but it has also inspired others to implement his process in their respective businesses with similarly successful results. As one of his early clients, my company was one of the first to benefit from his accountability systems, which drove efficiencies in every aspect of our business. *No Try! Only Do* is the reason we've continued to crush our competition, and if you want to have similar results, read *No Try! Only Do*."

Joe Freedman
founder/president, Music City Tents & Events

"Bailey nails it. Don't be upset with the results you didn't get because of the work you didn't do. *No Try! Only Do* is a blueprint on how the top 3 percent get it done over and over again."

John R. DiJulius III
author of *The Customer Service Revolution*

"The processes that Petra brought to our management team helped us define our culture and what our objectives as a company were going to be going forward. With well-defined objectives in hand and an understanding of who we were as an organization, our entire company began to march in sync toward the same goal—each employee realizing their individual responsibility in achieving our mission. Although our 750+ employees are located geographically across the country, Petra's disciplined approach to communication, alignment, and accountability helped us operate as a single unit."

Harry Fisk
CEO, EnduraCare Acute Care Services, LLC

"Moving your business to the *next level* requires vision, focus, and a deep well of grit. Andy's book will help you nail up your game in all three areas. *No Try! Only Do* is all about getting the job done right, time after time. I've had the pleasure of benefiting from Andy's sage counsel as a client of Petra Coach for several years and believe that readers of this book will gain valuable insights into systems and processes that Andy has proven to drive results. This is hard work. Andy can be your guide if you let him, but you must be ready to break with the past and embrace a new way of thinking about yourself as a leader and about your business. This book will walk you through how to truly focus on a small number of things, get your team aligned, build an awesome culture, and then tie it all together with accountability to results. I wish I had this book in my back pocket years ago and am excited about the impact it will have for leaders who choose to read and implement it."

Amith Nagarajan
founder/CEO, Aptify

"This book and the accountability tools that the Petra team bring to the table have been changing lives at TMC since we started implementing them. It has allowed us to build repeatable systems that work. People know where they are going and how to get there. It has given us the courage to face hard issues head-on that in the past we just ignored in hopes that they would go away. The same system has brought improvements to my personal life as well that will have an everlasting effect. 'Routine will set you free.'"

Jeff Turner
founder/CEO, Turner Machine Co., Inc.

"Entrepreneurs can get caught up in the whirlwind of being *busy.* We strongly believe in being purposeful about what you want to accomplish, applying laser-like focus, and getting it done. Andy Bailey helped us get better at that process through his coaching. I was very excited to see that he had captured those best practices in written form, and after reading it, I would highly recommend it to any entrepreneur working to get better. We still use the principles that Andy taught us today and refer to them often. It will be the same with the concepts covered in this book."

Chad Dudley
Managing Partner of Dudley DeBosier Injury Lawyers

"Andy Bailey has a unique way of putting the Rockefeller Habits into practical use in any organization, of any size, in any industry. He has brought me clarity and intentionality in my business and decisions. Since engaging with Petra, my entire team is pulling in the same direction, and we are seeing the results in our top and bottom line."

Vicki Hill
founder/CEO Mosaic Consulting Group

"Andy is a rare and special person one meets in life—someone who integrates what he believes, what he does, and how he treats others. A natural outcome is being a great coach and business leader. His journey of success in leading his first growth company of scale (NationLink) is the foundation of credibility, practicality, and confidence from which this book flows, sharing principles, stories, and tools to help growth company leaders also live a journey of purposeful, enjoyable success."

Keith Cupp
CEO, Gravitas International Coaching Association

"In the few years that I've known Andy Bailey, I've been challenged to move from where I was, an *accidental entrepreneur* (who knew almost nothing about business and scaling my company), to where I am today, a *No Try! Only Do* leader of a top-producing, committed team.

If you are looking for reasons (excuses) for your missteps and failures, this book is not for you. If you are seeking blunt, undeniable wisdom, proven principals, and no excuses, Andy's no-nonsense approach to business principals is presented in digestible bites for entrepreneurs at any stage of their journey. If you are ready to stop making excuses and start living your dreams, pick up your highlighter, open your mind, and get ready to change your life. *No Try! Only Do*."

Jen Zweiacker
founder/CEO, ZA Realty

"A must-read for entrepreneurs that *will* achieve their dreams. In *No Try! Only Do,* Andy takes us through a journey of his life philosophy on how to get things done by leveraging his life guidelines: purpose, alignment and accountability, and a road map for you to achieve your dreams."

Daniel A Marcos
CEO and cofounder, Growth Institute

"Andy Bailey and the Petra team make *it* happen—whatever your *it* may be. Implementing their consistency, organization, and accountability is a must in every growth-oriented business, and the only thing better than this book is working with Andy and his exceptional team, while building your own, and taking your business to whatever level you desire."

Robert D. Frankfather
D.P.M., CEO, Advanced Foot & Ankle

"Andy's book is a must-read for any entrepreneur wanting to truly grow their company the right way. The leverage you'll get from his tools related to staying focused around your core purpose, alignment of team members, and driving accountability will bring every company to greater heights."

Cameron Herold
founder, COO Alliance, author of *Double Double* and *Meetings Suck*

"I've read far too many business books that tell me how to think and far too few that tell me what to do. Andy's relentless calls to action have irritated me and my team for years ... and have also made our organization profoundly more successful. It's not the thinking, it's the doing. Thanks Andy!"

David S. Waddell
president, CEO, chief investment strategist
Waddell & Associates, LLC.

NO TRY ONLY DO.

NO TRY
ONLY DO.

BUILDING A BUSINESS ON
PURPOSE, ALIGNMENT, and ACCOUNTABILITY

ANDY BAILEY

Published by Advantage, Charleston, South Carolina.
Member of Advantage Media Group.

ADVANTAGE is a registered trademark, and the Advantage colophon is a trademark of Advantage Media Group, Inc.

Printed in the United States of America.

10 9 8 7 6 5 4 3

ISBN: 978-1-59932-683-2
LCCN: 2017936123

Cover and layout design by George Stevens.

This publication is designed to provide accurate and authoritative information in regard to the subject matter covered. It is sold with the understanding that the publisher is not engaged in rendering legal, accounting, or other professional services. If legal advice or other expert assistance is required, the services of a competent professional person should be sought.

TreeNeutral

Advantage Media Group is proud to be a part of the Tree Neutral® program. Tree Neutral offsets the number of trees consumed in the production and printing of this book by taking proactive steps such as planting trees in direct proportion to the number of trees used to print books. To learn more about Tree Neutral, please visit **www.treeneutral.com.**

Advantage Media Group is a publisher of business, self-improvement, and professional development books. We help entrepreneurs, business leaders, and professionals share their Stories, Passion, and Knowledge to help others Learn & Grow. Do you have a manuscript or book idea that you would like us to consider for publishing? Please visit **advantagefamily.com** or call **1.866.775.1696.**

To my bride—Nicole Bailey.

You saw me through everything in this book and more. You work tirelessly right beside me, building me up and making me a better person along the way. You always believe in me even in those times when I don't believe in myself. You give me stability and show me paths to significance. You stay positive in all those times that I need just a little extra positive. Thank you for being my partner in life and in business. Love you MTTY.

PREFACE: THE PUZZLE

What is the *first* thing you do when you put a puzzle together?

Most people say, "Start with the corners." Others say, "Dump all the pieces out," and still others say, "Put all the pieces right side up." But every now and then someone will say, "Look at the picture on the box."

Yes! Look at the picture on the box.

A puzzle is much easier to put together if you know how it's supposed to look. The Rockefeller Habits, the One-Page Strategic Plan, the Meeting Rhythms, the Petra Process—all of it is centered around everyone clearly understanding what the picture of the business looks like at certain points in the future so teams can make the best choices yearly, quarterly, monthly, weekly, daily, and hourly. A clear picture guides everyone to put the pieces together in the right way to achieve that result.

Doesn't it make more sense to create that clear picture and then communicate that picture of the business result so that each person puts the puzzle together faster?

I didn't learn lessons nearly enough via listening to others until I hit my own wall—again and again until it finally hurt badly enough. My hope is that my story will help you avoid some of the lessons I learned via bloody encounters. Today at Petra Coach we spend all of our time with teams, leaving lessons for them—to shortcut the path to success. I should have started much earlier than I did. I regret that.

"Motivation is what gets you started. Habit is what keeps you going."

JIM ROHN, ENTREPRENEUR AND MOTIVATIONAL SPEAKER

TABLE OF CONTENTS

PETRA COACH CASE STUDIES

FOREWORD

---

by Verne Harnish

author of *Mastering the Rockefeller Habits: What You Must Do to Increase the Value of Your Growing Firm; The Greatest Business Decisions of All Time;* and *Scaling Up: How a Few Companies Make It ... and Why the Rest Don't (Rockefeller Habits 2.0)*

"A great coach can lead you to a place where you don't need him anymore."

ANDRE AGASSI

No one has ever achieved peak performance without a coach. I've said this time and again, both in my book *Scaling Up* and in the many speeches and seminars I do every year, but the repetition doesn't dilute the raw truth.

Star athletes instinctively understand the need for a coach, and leaders of the world's largest organizations embrace coaching as a necessity. Many great entrepreneurs do, too, recognizing it as one of the most important investments a business can make at any stage.

As Andy Bailey, founder of Petra Coach, explains in *No Try! Only Do,* business leaders need someone who has been there, who has seen the chaos and felt the fear and frustration that, if left unchecked, can suck the life out of an organization. They need someone to hold their feet to the fire, to ask the tough questions, and to hold them accountable as they're challenged to perform at a higher level. They need an advocate—someone on the outside who can identify where leadership is choking off its own growth and can distinguish what their team can do to help them thrive. That is especially true when they are embarking on a scale-up.

Do you need a coach? Bailey, a gifted coach in his own right, will show you how to determine the answer and, if so, how to get the most out of a coaching relationship. *No Try! Only Do* makes clear the best way to work with a coach to create your own successful organization, detailing the people and processes you need to get there.

Success belongs to those with an insatiable desire to learn and an unquenchable bias for action. Are you going to improve or are you going to watch while other business leaders make their greatest goals happen? If you are determined to lead your business to its full potential, Bailey will show you the way.

VERNE HARNISH

founder, Entrepreneurs' Organization

founder, Association of Collegiate Entrepreneurs

founder, "Birthing of Giants" leadership program at the Massachusetts Institute of Technology

cofounder and principal of Gazelles Growth Institute and Gazelles International

author, *Mastering the Rockefeller Habits; The Greatest Business Decisions of All Time; Scaling Up: How a Few Companies Make It...and Why the Rest Don't (Rockefeller Habits 2.0)*

ACKNOWLEDGMENTS

Think about every good thing you have in your life—everything you love. Chances are it came as a direct result of friendship. Someone you know or knew opened a door, made an introduction, gave you insights, gave you something that lead you to something you love.

At *Petra Coach we are big on appreciation.* If you know us at all you know that we have a core value of "Please and Thank You: say it and mean it," and we coach our member companies to do the same. We believe that appreciation for another human being and what they have given is in short supply in this world, and it's our role, as members of the human race, to change that. Here are a few of the people that I want to recognize for making me a better human being and giving me the ability to write this book.

NICOLE BAILEY (my bride)—No one on this list deserves more of my appreciation than you. You have been with me on this crazy journey since day one, through all the ups and downs and twists and turns. You are my compass—thank you.

MADISON AND GRACEN BAILEY (my daughters)—Wow. You two continue to surprise and amaze me. You, without knowing it, have given me perspective on life—perspective of what's important and what's not quite so important. I could not be more proud of the adults you are growing up to be—thank you.

RON AND DEBORAH BAILEY—Dad, my entrepreneurship drive grew from you. Watching and sometimes working around you inspired me to take my own path and make my own way in life. Deborah, you give to others more than anyone I know and have set an example that I forever will be striving to achieve—thank you.

GWEN AND CHUCK ROTHAUSER—Mom, I wish you were here to experience this with me, but I know you are watching over us with the sun shining on your shoulders and a smile on your face; I think of you often. Chuck, you are an inspiration to me and my family. I have witnessed a form of true love from you for my mother that gave me a new appreciation for life—thank you.

MY GRANDPARENTS (Aaron and Louise Bailey / Jessie and Paul Warren)—You taught me the meaning of hard work and perseverance. My home is filled with images that remind me of each of you and how you shaped me in my youth—thank you.

MY BROTHER AND SISTERS (Bonita Nolan, Cameron Bailey, Brooke Bailey)—Siblings shape each other in ways that many times aren't noticeable for years. Having you as part of my journey makes it more meaningful and certainly more enjoyable—thank you.

MY EO FORUM (Arnie Malham, Joe Freedman, David Waddell, Steve Curnutte, Sonny Clark, Clay Blevins, Rob Frankfather)—Boys, for years we have met monthly to discuss our wins and losses but mostly to have one another's backs in life. If I were able to pick my band of brothers it would be you seven men. You have made me think, made me listen, made me move, made me appreciate, made me laugh, and made me cry—thank you.

THE NATIONLINK TEAM (Andrew, Angela, Bethany, Brian, Brooke, Christian, Gary, George, David, Jeff, Jennifer, Jessica, Joel, Julie R., Julie T., Justin, Kim, Lisa F., Lisa S., Mike, Mistie, Nathan, Nicole J., Robert, Shawn, Shonda, Stacey, Stephen, Teresa, Thomas, Todd, Victor D., Victor M., Wendy, Zachary)—My time with you was a time of change. Each of you gave me the space, the patience, and the inspiration to change and grow—thank you.

THE PETRA TEAM Some of us have worked together for a decade or more and some of you are brand new to the team, but each of you bring it all every day to make this place "work" and I am better because of you—thank you.

THE PETRA COACHES Tens of thousands of team members are better people because of the tireless energy you bring to each planning day. I am continually impressed and inspired by each of you; you keep me on my toes and are a catalyst for my improvement—thank you.

THE ALIGN TEAM A simple online tool that grew from an idea and a piece of notebook paper. You guys created and continue to create a shift toward focus in so many, including myself—thank you.

THE GAZELLES COUNCIL Leadership is earned, and this group has certainly earned that title from me. I appreciate being a part of this group that I learn so much from—thank you.

ENTREPRENEURS' ORGANIZATION (EO)—Over twenty years ago I walked into my first EO event and found my tribe. Thank you for always making me feel welcome, opening new doors of opportunity, and teaching me so much—thank you.

BOG CLASS OF 2008—Three years of learning, growing, and laughing together set me on a course of self-discovery that continues today. Lifelong friends from every corner of the planet—thank you.

VERNE HARNISH—Your teachings changed my life in many ways. This entire book was born from what I have learned as a result of that first workshop many years ago—thank you.

ROBERT WAGNON—You believed in me when I didn't believe in myself and gave me the fuel to get out of my own way—thank you.

JACK DALY—You set a high standard and encouraged me to "up my game and walk my talk"—thank you.

RALEIGH (my dog)—Unconditional love. Always the first to greet me with off-the-chart levels of enthusiasm after a long trip or just at the end of the day. My running partner and shotgun rider—thank you.

ALL of the authors, thinkers, leaders, friends, and mentors that have given me time, attention, and love over my lifetime—thank you.

THE PETRA COACH EXPERIENCE

"If you don't like change, you'll like irrelevance even less!"

**US ARMY GENERAL
ERIC KEN SHINSEKI, RET.**

Experts don't exist—or at least, they shouldn't self-identify.

The people worth knowing in this world are the ones who are always seeking additional knowledge to improve. They consider themselves to be students of life rather than experts.

As a student myself, I didn't write this book to be the definitive guide to anything. Instead, *No Try! Only Do* is the combination of knowledge gathered from more than fifteen hundred days in planning sessions; well over ten thousand hours coaching CEOs, executives, and leaders; and speaking in front of enough total people to fill Madison Square Garden multiple times over. It's the lessons learned implementing Verne Harnish's Rockefeller Habits, as they've been molded to drive the efficiency, profitability, and culture of drastically different businesses, including my own.

Our coaching firm, Petra Coach (www.PetraCoach.com), guides teams to build businesses on solid foundations, and our software, Align (www.AlignToday.com), keeps everyone on track toward achieving their ultimate goal, however big and audacious it may be, with our team tying it all together to deliver the experience that businesses need to create much-needed change.

We live the Rockefeller Habits as much as we train others to do the same. We're continually learning and seeking to improve in everything we do—an attitude that firmly supports our mission: **to eliminate the attitude of "try" from teams and inspire them to do anything by leveraging the power of purpose, alignment, and accountability.**

Our six core values—those beliefs and principles that drive our behavior every day at Petra Coach—support that core purpose. Just as we tell the companies we coach, we've got to define our own core purpose and core values before we can even think about leading, managing, or coaching someone else. Just as on an airplane that's rapidly losing cabin pressure, you have to put on your own oxygen mask first before you can help others.

OUR CORE VALUES

THERE IS *NO TRY! ONLY DO* ... (THE TITLE OF THIS BOOK)

At Petra Coach we don't make excuses—we make progress. We look at each challenge as a new level of growth that only makes each of us better. Nothing is left undone here; we finish what we start and we do what we say—we don't try. We seek guidance and advice, not step-by-step instruction. We also believe that language is important and you won't catch us using the word "try" in any context.

I'VE GOT YOUR BACK, NO MATTER WHAT.

At Petra Coach no one is in it for himself or herself. We sacrifice for one another to achieve more than we can alone. This is no place for seeking praise, placing blame, or being a prima donna. All of us will at one time or another find ourselves in a spot that we truly need another team member and by living this value, we always "know" that a team member will be there.

"PLEASE" AND "THANK YOU": SAY AND MEAN IT.

At Petra Coach, we recognize the power of appreciation and being nice. We say *please* when asking and say *thank you* when it's deserved—which is often. We use handwritten notes and the spoken word to express these basic levels of respect. We "seek out" moments that team members perform in a way that we can recognize them and we act on them.

EVERYTHING IS AN EXPERIENCE, EVERY TIME.

At Petra Coach we make each interaction an experience. We ask ourselves how we can add an extra 15 percent on top of what we have already done that would make someone say, "Wow, that was an experience," "That was more than I expected," "I want to do this again," and then tell others about it. With one another, with our members, with our vendors, and even with the mail carrier. Everything is an experience to be remembered and remarked about.

SEE AROUND THE CURVES: ANTICIPATE NEEDS AND PRE-FILL THEM.

At Petra Coach a big part of work involves us seeing what is coming before it arrives. In planning sessions with teams; in traveling via planes, trains, and automobiles; and as importantly with one another. Far before the moment arrives, we think through what is coming and work to be prepared at a level most would consider overboard. By doing this we are uber-prepared and gain the ability to respond with more agility than everyone else. We pay ultra-attention to what is being said and what is not being said in every interaction to "see" what is coming next.

BE CURIOUS: ASK "WHY" AND IMPROVE.

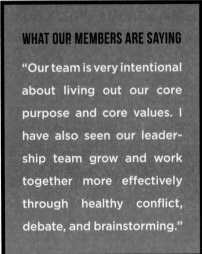

WHAT OUR MEMBERS ARE SAYING

"Our team is very intentional about living out our core purpose and core values. I have also seen our leadership team grow and work together more effectively through healthy conflict, debate, and brainstorming."

At Petra Coach we never feel like we know everything and have arrived. We never accept things as they are. We seek constant improvement in ourselves, in those around us, in our process, in everything. We ask, "Why does it need to be done this way?" and seek ways to improve. We never stop, as we know when we do, it's over.

NEW HABITS

This book is about the winding and sometimes broken road I wandered down as a young entrepreneur. It's about frustration, fear, failure, hard-fought success, and learning to suck up my pride and get out of my own way. It's about the businesses Petra Coach has worked with over the years and how they've embraced the difficult road of change, holding onto the Rockefeller Habits methodologies until they become foundational habits of their companies and their teams.

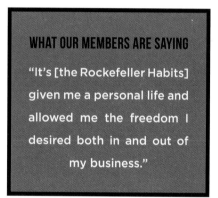

WHAT OUR MEMBERS ARE SAYING

"It's [the Rockefeller Habits] given me a personal life and allowed me the freedom I desired both in and out of my business."

It's also about freedom—the freedom to spend your time on strategy instead of putting out day-to-day fires, to enjoy your life instead of just your life inside the business, and the freedom to allow others to flourish in their talents, driving positive change and growth in your business. You can do it, but you must be ready and you must be willing to work for it, because you must *want* to change for change to occur. You may be frustrated with your current structure (or lack thereof) or fearful of missing an opportunity without a solid foundation on which to grow. If you're not frustrated or afraid—if you're thinking right now, "Nope, I'm good"—then don't read any further!

Certainly only contact us about coaching if you have the overwhelming desire to change in order to grow. If not, there's nothing anyone can do for you.

Creating new habits isn't easy, but worthwhile things are never easy.

This book has two parts: the **long version (p. 10)** and the **short version (p. 117)**. If you'd like to learn about my personal experiences, how I first discovered the Rockefeller Habits, and how implementing them in my business was the deciding factor in its success, then keep reading—that's what the first part is all about.

If you're a "D" on the DiSC* assessment like me, however, you probably just want to get to the point: Why Petra Coach? That's the short version; go straight to the case studies and find out how several uniquely different companies have benefitted from the Petra process.

In the long version, you'll also get a closer look at the coach-selection process and what a day with Petra Coach might look like. It's a choose-your-own-adventure kind of book, with a little bit for everyone, from D to C.

Questions? Check us out at www.PetraCoach.com. ❧

---

*See next page for definition of DiSC assessment.

GLOSSARY OF COMMON TERMS USED IN THIS BOOK

Actions for Core Values, Purpose, and BHAG™	Once you have defined your core values, core purpose, and BHAG, it's time to take "actions" in your business to ensure that everyone (1) knows what they are, (2) understands what they mean, and (3) lives them every day and in every way. These should be actionable things that a person or a group can go and do to support your business's overall values, purpose, and BHAG.
Annual Initiatives	These should be big company priorities/initiatives that take all year to complete, impact the business in significant ways, and drive the business toward hitting its targets while not straying too far from the revenue line.
BHAG©	Big Hairy Audacious Goal. Your BHAG should be a long-term, ten-to-thirty-year, very big goal. It should be inspiring—just short of a "save the planet from destruction" statement.
Brand Promise	Strategic anchors—the three ways you matter to your customers and that make you different from the competition. Examples of strategic anchors include: McDonald's—speed, consistency, fun for kids; Southwest Airlines—low fares, lots of flights, lots of fun.
Core Purpose	This is the "why" of your business—the real reason that you do what you do. It is the reason that you get up each morning and it is the reason that others in your business should as well. The core purpose is your business's contribution to making a difference.
Core Values	These are the "How we deliver solutions, service, product, etc. ..." They are a handful of rules that drive and define decisions in the organization.
DiSC	An invaluable personal-assessment tool used to increase productivity, teamwork, and communication in organizations and the growth of your business.
Key Thrusts/Capabilities	Thinking in terms of key thrusts/capabilities, we can define a short list of items (three to five) that we need to be very good at (capabilities) in order to hit our targets. These can be around hiring, sales, operations, or anything you wish.
LER	Labor efficiency ratio. For every dollar we spend on labor, how many dollars do we return to the business? This metric is a powerful way to manage productivity in any business.
One-on-Ones	Also called "two-weekers" or "tweekers," these are meetings between a team member and his/her supervisor held biweekly as a check-in for both participants regarding their business and personal lives.
Opportunities	Right now, these are the things that take time but not too much time, and if we took advantage of them, we could wildly exceed our stated plan. For example, "We could take advantage of these over the next twenty-four months."

OPPP	One-Page Personal Plan. A single sheet of paper designed in a way to allow a person to easily define their personal life goals in four areas (relationships, achievements, rituals, and wealth).
OPSP	One-Page Strategic Plan. A single sheet of paper designed in a way to allow a business to easily define the strategy and execution points for the business.
Petra	Latin for "rock" and the name of our coaching practice.
Priorities	The few most important items that you can work toward achieving in a given time period; sometimes referred to as goals.
Rockefeller Habits	Business operating methodologies rooted in the practices of John D. Rockefeller with pillars of "Priorities," "Data," and "Rhythm" that support the growth of business.
SMART	Specific, measurable, attainable, relative/relevant, time-bound.
Sandbox/ Ideal Client	Sandbox (1) geographic region: where they are located; (2) primary solution: what exactly they are buying; and (3) market / distribution channel / client type—what they look like (size, revenue, team, square footage, etc.)
Strengths	Right now, those things that your business does better than others and that your clients care about. Be specific. If you feel the *team* is a strength, then think about what it is "about" the team that is the actual strength. If you feel *technology* is a strength, then think about what it is "about" the technology that is the actual strength.
SWOT	Strengths, weaknesses, opportunities, and threats (SWOT) is a dynamic worksheet updated every quarter by all participants and particularly leadership.
Threats	Right now, those things that your business needs to watch closely and mitigate as much as possible. Threats are things that could cause you to dramatically miss your revenue targets or even put you out of business.
Three-to-Five-Year Targets	These should be the most important things you are measuring and watching. Typically, metrics like revenue, gross margin, profit, and number of locations make the list, but this is specific to your business.
Topgrading	The practice of creating the highest quality workforce by ensuring that talent acquisition and talent management processes focus on identifying, hiring, promoting, and retaining high performers, A Players, in the organization at every salary level.
Weaknesses	Right now, those things that are slowing down progress, creating issues, or simply just need some attention. Be specific. If you feel sales is a weakness, think about what is it "about" sales that is the actual weakness. If you feel location is a weakness, think about what is it "about" the location that is the actual weakness.

THE LONG VERSION

GROWING THROUGH
THE ROCKS

CHAPTER 1

EARLY LESSONS IN ENTREPRENEURSHIP

t's the gift and curse of entrepreneurs to see gaps everywhere.

Most of us entrepreneurs walk around this planet constantly spotting these gaps and thinking, "Oh, there's a gap. That process could be done better, this could be more efficient, and if we do it this way, someone might pay for it. How do we build a business around that?"

My youngest daughter, Gracen, is a great example of this. At age fifteen she saw a gap in people having extra stuff in their homes and not having the time or expertise to sell it on eBay.

It started with my own growing collection of outdated Fitbits. I got the first version when it came out, then I wanted the next one and the next and never got rid of the old ones—they just sat there collecting dust in my closet. So Gracen sold them for me and at the same time learned how to negotiate the posting, bidding, selling, and shipping processes at eBay.

She could have just done that for me, made a few bucks, and left it at that. But she saw a gap—she saw the need to help others sell items that they didn't want to just throw away but didn't have the time to sell.

It was the beginning of "Gracie's Garage," and the very first thing she did was create a list of item types that sold well and for high multiples. Then she created a flyer and had me hand it to people who I thought could use her services.

In a couple months, she'd taken over the big walk-in closet in our guest bedroom. Everything in it is labeled and inventoried, neatly organized into drawers, and logs kept on their online activity. She does the research, handles the shipping, and even negotiates the complaint and refund process if buyers receive an item that's either not what they wanted, missing a part, or broken.

There are plenty of nights when I come home, walk by the closet, and hear her playing music and typing away, digging into the history of some item or communicating with someone on the other side of the world.

And just like an entrepreneur, she gets frustrated. When she first started selling, she came to me in a huff because eBay was charging her three dollars to process a payment.

"That's three of my dollars," she said angrily.

I couldn't have been prouder.

She's learning these incredible lessons at a young age, and even though they're on a small level now, they'll lead her down a path that will help her be a better entrepreneur later on; and she's already pretty good at it.

My own business, a cellular phone agency called Nation-Link, was also pretty good at spotting entrepreneurial gaps and filling them. For instance, we took a unique approach to billing in 2004 that brought us an incredible number of new clients.

Even today, wireless bills are a confusing mess, and you can imagine the complexity of a one- to three-person family plan versus the monthly bill for an organization with fifteen or even five hundred phones. Often, people just gave up trying to sort them out and simply paid the bill.

We saw that as a gap and decided to tackle it from two directions: creating a bill-auditing service and creating an online portal that allowed an organization to handle all things cellular in one place.

For the bill auditing, we'd review companies' cell-phone statements and then report back to them on where they could save money, such as changing from one plan to another, and cutting out unused services and other unnecessary expenses.

I recall one organization in Alabama that we ended up saving close to $16,000 a month on their wireless bill. Such extra money drops straight to the bottom line of an organiza-tion, and it costs them little for us to do it, since we just took our fee out of their savings as a percentage.

At the same time, this allowed us to get our foot in the door with companies. We became a trusted partner, and when they looked to purchase new wireless services in the future, they came to us.

The second part, the online portal, came out of the necessity for these companies to get everything they needed, such as new phones and accessories for employees, as well as one-stop billing management. A business could see their bill, how much NationLink saved them through bill auditing, and what they'd expect to pay on their next bill. Then they could place orders, and we'd ship whatever they needed directly to them, maximizing revenue per employee on *our* team at the same time.

Petra Coach,[1] too, was created to fill the gap between what Verne Harnish's "Rockefeller Habits" are and how you actually put them into practice in your business. Our software, Align,[2] was another stopgap that's proven highly useful to businesses, whether or not they're implementing the Habit methodologies.

This need for guidance on how to bring these innovative business practices off the pages of Harnish's *Mastering the Rockefeller Habits* and into practical practice is the origin of Petra Coach. Because as much as the concepts are laid out and well described in the book, the implementation process is not easy and it's unique for every business.

I discovered this when I put the Habits into practice in my own business and when others came to me later, asking if I could help their business in implementing them.

This is where Petra Coach coaching comes in. We don't do the Rockefeller Habits for you; we coach from our own entrepreneurial experiences and hundreds of hours of training, leading you and your team to put them into practice, holding

---

1   Petra Coach, www.PetraCoach.com, works directly with businesses to implement the "Rockefeller Habits" and other operational methodologies to improve performance.

2   Align, www.aligntoday.com, is an online platform. To see more about Align, read chapter 4 or visit www.PetraCoach.com/resources/align.

you accountable, and helping everyone stick with it until the Rockefeller Habits become just that: everyday, functioning, effective, business-growing habits.

But Petra Coach, and later Align—the software we created to fill the gap of tracking and aligning team members in real-time—were not early ventures for me in the entrepreneurial world. I first had to build a business, sell it, take it back, and struggle to build it again before I discovered the Rockefeller Habits—and even then I had to figure them out for myself. It was twenty years, in fact, before the idea for Petra Coach hit me like a rock.

ENTREPRENEURIAL FROM A YOUNG AGE

> "It takes twenty years to make
> an overnight success."
>
> **EDDIE CANTOR**

I've worked in plenty of jobs in my life but never in what you'd call a career. I've always been an entrepreneur, even as a young kid.

One of my first entrepreneurial ventures was in book sales. I was seven years old when I struck on the idea that I could sell my books and turn a pure profit. I stacked my collection of *Winnie the Pooh*, Dr. Seuss, and the like as high as I could in my Radio Flyer and began going door-to-door selling them.

I got in big trouble when my mom found out about that, but that was the first time I remember setting out and essentially starting my own business.

Around the age of twelve, I hit on a more legit way of making money—selling mistletoe over the holidays. A friend and I would scale the tall pine trees that grew near where we lived in Charleston, South Carolina, and harvest the mistletoe growing in the branches. We'd put those cuttings in little baggies and sell them door-to-door for one dollar each. It was a lot of work, and looking back on it, it was probably pretty dangerous, but we made some good pocket money doing it—at least enough to buy extra-large Icees at the 7-Eleven convenience store down the street.

Of course, I also did the normal things kids do to make some extra money—cutting grass, pulling weeds, and other yard work that the neighbors would pay me a few bucks to do.

Then, when I was old enough to get on a payroll, I picked up all kinds of gigs, from working on a riverboat over the summer to cleaning toilets in factories. Nothing was ever beneath me.

But I never had a job that I wanted to keep long term. I was more interested in creating my own path, so to speak.

TAKING A DIFFERENT DIRECTION

Right after I graduated from high school, I went to Middle Tennessee State University (MTSU). I was seventeen years old at the time, and I didn't even make it through my first year because I realized that I didn't do well with something I couldn't see results in. Immature thinking, for sure, but there it was.

The thing is, I was never interested in school. I was disruptive and got in a little trouble. I'm sure a good part of that disinterest was because we moved around a lot after my parents got divorced when I was six, and each new school had its own "hazing" process—or whatever you call it when a bunch of boys chase the new kid into a locker room stall and beat the crap out of him. But I also had problems with authority. I couldn't stand to be told to do something I didn't want to do.

In fact, it was the last straw for my mom when, at age fourteen, I threw a chair across my classroom, because I didn't want to read Steinbeck's *The Red Pony.*

They sent me to the principal's office for that one, and by the time I got home my mom had already called my dad.

"You've got to come get him," she said, and that was that.

Living with my dad ended the long string of moving around the country for me, but it didn't change my attitude about authority. MTSU didn't let me come back after that first year, so I left formal education and took a job in construction.

For a year and a half I built houses. Not just framing either, but the whole house from the foundation up.

This was back when subcontracting of plumbers, electricians, or roofers wasn't as common as it is today. It was just the four of us digging the footers, pouring the concrete, framing the house, putting in windows, and even building the cabinets. For me, it was a "learn as you go" experience, and most of the time I did a decent job; other times, though … not so much.

One day as we were putting siding on a new house, the boss came over and told me to help install the plumbing.

"I don't know how to do plumbing," I said, surprised.

"All you need to know about plumbing is that shit runs downhill and payday is on Friday," he said. "Now go plumb the house."

I did it, and when I was done it looked terrible—but it was functional.

Construction wasn't something I wanted to make a career out of, but that job taught me a lot about physical labor, hard work, and how much you can actually endure in the blazing summer heat of Mid-Tennessee. I stuck it out for a while, and then eventually decided to start my own landscaping company.

Today I know a lot of entrepreneurs who started out with their own lawn care or landscaping business. Apparently, it's pretty common.

It wasn't a career move for me, but it was a step in the right direction. I was my own boss and made my own very long hours. I cut grass for a while, built some decks, and fences; I even went so far as to put the company name on some t-shirts. That lasted for about two years until I finally decided to go back to school and work on my education.

They let me back into MTSU, and even though in the end I left lacking a semester to graduate, the best thing that came out of it was meeting my wife, Nicole. It was there, too, that we started a little business together in the attic of our house: a business that would be my love and curse for the next eighteen years.

IN THE BAG

Do you remember bag phones? If you do, you either had one or you remember your parents talking on one in the car, the bulky black bag taking up half the front passenger seat, and the connection so bad that the most commonly shouted non-swear word in the car was, "What?"

Before I started that small attic-based business, my job was selling bag phones and hardwired car phones. And I made pretty good money at it. By senior year, I was making six figures as a top-producing straight-commission contracted sales rep.

The challenge was that I could never stop. If I took a day off, I was losing money so I just kept going, burning the candle on both ends as I managed some degree of schoolwork and sales at the same time.

No one taught me about the concept of "residual sales" or "subscription-based business," but I realized that this need to always be selling was not sustainable. I needed to create a business that allowed me to do the work once and create a regular income stream.

At this point it was the early 1990s and Nicole and I had two thoughts on our minds: getting married and starting a business. For me, getting a business going took priority, since I wanted to have that regular income stream in place before I even thought about starting a family.

Then it occurred to me that the business I was already in had a blatant gap in it—and it centered around pagers.

The cell organization I contracted with had fooled around with pagers a bit, but it wasn't their primary focus. What intrigued me about them was that you could sell a pager once and then get paid for it month after month without having to constantly, actively work for that income. So we set out to build a paging organization and wound up building a pretty strong subscription-based business in a very short period of time.

PAGING DR. OPPORTUNITY

The model is simple. You've got the carrier, which is the organization that owns the tower systems and infrastructure, and you have the customer. Between the two, there's a third party that sets up your pager service and provides customer service. That third party pays the carrier $1.50 or so for a pager number once a month, then turns around and sells that number to somebody else for $10 or $15 a month. That's pretty good arbitrage between those two figures. Do that with a few thousand customers and you're set—and that's what we did.

Of course, we weren't the only ones who thought of this. There were dozens if not hundreds of other third parties already out there, buying numbers and setting up services. What we did was find the *gap* in the industry.

At the time, if you wanted a pager, you stood in line at a store or pager carrier location in some urban setting to purchase it and get it activated. On top of that, if you lived in a rural area and wanted a pager, you had to drive to the big city just so you could stand in line, buy the pager, and activate it. Our model allowed us to push the product into those rural areas where people could buy a pager off the shelf and activate it by calling our 1-800 number—a subscription model that wasn't being done at the time.

By 1994, we were signing up agent distributors in rural markets from Kentucky to Alabama and were one of the very first businesses to have kiosks in malls, launching our first one in the former Bellevue Center in Nashville, along with our own retail stores.

As our retail locations grew, so did our overhead. We had to get product in and out of those stores and kiosks, so we started to work in the cellular side of the business as well, offering cell phones along with pagers through our distribution models.

Everything was working well. Our recurring revenue was growing and our customer base was in the tens of thousands only a few years after launching the organization, which we'd named NationLink Paging, later changing it to NationLink Wireless once we started including cellular phones.

Then, sometime in 1998, a guy walked into my office and offered me more money than I'd ever seen in my life for the paging business.

And I ignored it.

ONE HELL OF A LIFE LESSON

That man offered Nicole and me multiple seven-figures just for the subscribers in our paging business, which he was simply going to roll into a larger customer base. I turned it down. I was told the business was worth much more than this figure and believed it.

We walked away from that deal and within a few months our subscription base began to dwindle as cell service became more reliable in these same rural areas. In a very short period of time, a large quantity of our pager numbers had been shut off and business had dipped sharply.

In hindsight, it was probably a good thing that I didn't take that money. I was thirty years old at the time—still really young. If I'd suddenly become a multi-millionaire, I don't know what I would have done, good or bad. I probably would have spent it, and I would have never learned that money is something you can either spend wastefully or use strategically to build real wealth.

ROUND ONE: SOLD

We finally did sell the business two years later to an organization that was looking to bundle subscribers and infrastructure into one business. They already owned towers and were looking to buy more, building out from the area they already covered between Nashville and Memphis in an attempt to offer coverage from north Kentucky down the Gulf Coast into Florida. In buying our organization, the plan was to move our thirty thousand or so subscribers onto their towers, then to sell pagers and cell phones in that geographic region using our sales and marketing methodologies.

When they first approached us, they were only offering pagers and didn't offer any cellular at all. They didn't know how to, and frankly, they didn't know the paging business very well, either. But we did.

We were always a good sales and marketing organization, and the plan was that we were going to train all of the new sales and marketing teams, run the retail stores, develop new sales channels, do the distribution, and manage all of this as a new business. It would grow from there and we'd gross more because we'd no longer have to pay a major carrier for its towers and infrastructure.

It was a really good idea. Trouble was they ran out of money before they could get around to actually paying us for our business.

I haven't shared this with many people but wanted to get this in the book—because it's part of me paying my business tuition. It sounds ludicrous to say now, but one of my most embarrassing acts in business was when I spent almost a year before we even got to the closing table building inventory, training salespeople, expanding the management team, and selling product for that organization. We even gave them our name—NationLink—and started an Internet service provider with modems that you could activate with a CD, like an early AOL or NetZero. We owned the US trademark to that name but still began to build it out in anticipation of joining that organization; that's how engrained I was in the process.

My lesson from all of this—run the business like it's never going to sell, right up until the wire transfer.

When it came time for the organization to purchase our business, we went through with it, closing on it with no financial exchange at the time. Instead, we took a note that basically said that the organization promised to start paying us within three months of the closing date.

We never saw a dime.

That experience is one I draw from to this day in the coaching process. If business owners working with us tell me about a poor business decision they made, in the past, I can not only relate but can usually one-up them. That's why our coaches at Petra Coach aren't your typical coaches—they all come from that school-of-hard-knocks background. They learned in the trenches of entrepreneurship, earned their stripes on the battlefield of business, and relate to our clientele on the grounds of mutual "I've been there, too" camaraderie, as opposed to learning solely in a classroom.

THE KNOWN IS BETTER THAN THE UNKNOWN

When our payments were continually missed, I finally went to the buyer to find out what was going on—the whole business was in complete disrepair. Relationships with vendors and subscribers had been sorely damaged, they owed money left and right, and they were flat broke.

We were left with a choice. We could walk away from NationLink, give it up as a loss, and start over again with a new name and all the pluses and minuses of building a new business from scratch, or we could take it back and fix what had been broken.

I say "we," because it wasn't a decision I wanted to make on my own. I needed to involve the management team and find out what they wanted to do, because without them, neither business would stand a chance.

On the Friday after I received the additional bad news from the buyer I invited the management team over to my house for a meeting. We sat down in the living room, opened up a few beers, and got right to the point.

"Okay, team," I said, "this is what we've got."

I explained everything, from what had happened to the deal to where it left us.

At the end of it, I looked at all of them and said, "So now we can go one of two routes. We can take route number one, which means Monday we all leave and go start a new organization, or we can take route two: talk to this guy and take NationLink back."

We already had a name for the new organization—Blue Rock Wireless—and office space we could use from a buddy of mine in downtown Nashville.

On the other hand, however, we all knew NationLink. We'd built the name from nothing and there was a good chance we could build it again. But it wouldn't be easy.

"If we take NationLink back," I said, "it's going to be tough. We'll all have to take pay cuts, but in two years I promise you'll be paid back any difference with interest."

The team thought it over. I had no idea how we were going to build it back up to the point where we could pay back lost salary plus interest in only two years, let alone reestablish a customer and vendor relationship base, but the consensus of the meeting was that the known is better than the unknown. Let's get NationLink back—we can build it again.

ROUND TWO: TAKING BACK THE BUSINESS

Even though the known was pretty shitty, it was known. We knew what needed to happen and we knew how to get there because we'd done it before; we were aware of what would be involved.

Still, it was a tough two years. The organization that bought us hadn't paid many bills during the short six months they controlled the business. We knew something was up even before I talked to the guy about taking the organization back—vendors were calling me, my wife, and even team members about overdue bills.

It made no sense. These were relationships we'd developed over years, and now these vendors were calling me left and right and asking, "Hey Andy, what's going on?"

It took a lot of phone calls and meetings to rebuild those relationships, and it was both embarrassing and overwhelmingly humbling to have to ask for help, but we still made those calls and communicated everything, good and bad.

We called vendors and said to each one, "Look, we've taken the organization back. You know us and you know we'll make this good. It's going to take a while for us to get caught up, and even though we don't have the money to pay you back now, we'll make it right. I promise."

I said that while literally not knowing how we were going to get out from under the hill of debt other than by working incredibly long hours, but they gave us the time we needed. They knew me, they knew our team, and they

CHAPTER 2

STRENGTHENING A NATION

wasn't looking for the Rockefeller Habits when I found them. I didn't even know that I should be looking for them when I did—and in fact, I couldn't tell you where I came across a copy of *Mastering the Rockefeller Habits* for the first time. But learning them and learning how to implement them was a life-changing experience. The Habits not only taught me how to vastly increase the value and profitability of NationLink, but it altered the course of my life.

My improvement journey started with a workshop in Nashville in 2004. Not long after we took NationLink back, I attended a daylong EO workshop that featured *Mastering the Rockefeller Habits* author, Verne Harnish. I'd read his book prior to the workshop and was already a fan of his methodologies, and this was a whole day spent learning how to implement the processes he presented in the book.

We worked through a lot of the components of the Habits that day, and afterward I walked away with a basic working knowledge on how to get them going in our business. We mulled over the ideas when we got back and talked about what might happen, but the big kick didn't happen until

2005, when I attended Verne's "Birthing of Giants" (BOG) program at MIT.

These days it's called the Entrepreneurial Master's Program, or EMP, but the BOG format hasn't changed much at all. It's an intense learning process that requires a three-year commitment. Every year you attend the program for four days in June. Speakers are on for two to three hours each, and Verne was always the kickoff speaker, laying the foundation for learning. One of my greatest life experiences was in 2016, going back for the Year One introduction of EMP as a speaker. It's truly humbling to give back to a program that gave me so much.

Back then, however, I remember being completely blown away during that first session, not just by the content but also by the attendees. There were sixty-five of us from all over the world, and only a few of us were from the United States. They were from every region on the planet, and I learned an incredible amount from my classmates. At the same time, I was getting an intense course in how to firmly implement the Rockefeller Habits and other business-improvement methodologies.

If that wasn't enough motivation, it was understood that very few of us would actually wind up doing everything we were being taught at BOG.

"Eighty-five percent of you will leave here and do nothing," we were told. "Fifteen percent of you will do something—but only four percent of you will do everything. Where are you going to fall?"

MAN, THIS IS HARD

I came back from that first BOG session with a passion. I was not going to be the majority. I was going to be that 4 percent! We already had a written one-page plan, which we'd begun after that first one-day workshop in Nashville, but now we were making the Habits happen. We started right away with the daily huddle and, man, was it hard. No one wanted to do it!

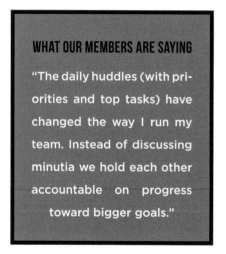

WHAT OUR MEMBERS ARE SAYING

"The daily huddles (with priorities and top tasks) have changed the way I run my team. Instead of discussing minutia we hold each other accountable on progress toward bigger goals."

But I was determined that we were going to do it, that we were going to implement all the Habits and follow the format Verne offered in the book, but we didn't have a coach. Hell, I didn't even know coaches existed back then—that you could hire someone from Verne's Rockefeller Habits coaching organization, Gazelles, to help you with this stuff. All I knew was that it was frustrating. I was frustrated, the team was frustrated, and everyone was complaining about the new system they were being made to follow.

I wasn't going to let frustration stop us, however, so I reached out to the man himself. I called Verne.

"This is not working," I told him. "People are not happy."

"It's hard," he said, but maybe he could help. He asked if he could listen in on the next daily huddle, so the next day I secretly put him on speakerphone during our short morning meeting. Afterward, I picked up the phone and asked him what he thought.

"You're doing fine," he said. "You've just got to keep doing it. In sixty days, it will be habit, and it will be a part of your organization forever. You just can't give up on it."

THE BAKING POWDER IN YOUR CHANGE BISCUIT

Ari Weinzweig, co-owner and founding partner of the Zing-erman's community of businesses, once gave a speech addressing why coming *together* for a group outcome is so important, and the way he put it really stuck with me ... much like a good biscuit.

Years later I got to see Ari speak, and his story brought more clarity to why the daily huddle is so important.

Ari opened Zingerman's Delicatessen in Ann Arbor, Michigan, in 1982, and over the next twenty years, grew it into a business model that generates more than $60 million in annual sales. But he didn't do it by building a bunch more delicatessens. Instead, he built a model so unique and suc-cessful that he started an organization called ZingTrain, dedicated solely to teaching others about the Zingerman's approach to business—and the secret to their sauce is something they call "Bottom Line Change."

"Bottom Line Change," said Ari, "Is a simple, clear, exceptionally effective process for creating compelling change in an organization of any size. It's a recipe we've refined and reused so many times that we've become just as good at making constructive change happen as we are at making chicken soup, because it applies across the board. In fact, we use it so often that most of us in the Zingerman's community know it by its acronym, BLC.

It's a simple recipe, but like any good recipe, it has incredible depth and versatility. Simply stated in a clear, linear fashion, the five steps to Bottom Line Change are:

1. Write a clear and compelling purpose for change—this is the "why" that's driving us to make changes in the first place.

2. Draft a positive vision for the future and develop leadership agreement on what's described in that vision.

3. Put together a microcosm—people chosen from all the various parts of the organization— who use their cultural expertise to develop a communication plan to tell everyone who will be affected by the impending change.

4. Tell everyone impacted and have them—i.e., the people who will do the actual work—develop an action plan to put the change into action.

5. Begin implementing the change. En route you'll want to regularly check progress, adjust the

action plan as needed, learn from mistakes, and celebrate successes when they occur.

Ari went on to describe each step in more depth, but the simplest step was the one that really stuck with me. When it comes to Bottom Line Change, you can have a clear-as-hell purpose, a great vision, and compelling processes, but if you try to tell others about it on your own—if you don't speak with people in your organization who represent those affected by the change and ask them to help create the communication plan—then chances are your hope for change is going to fall through the cracks.

Or, as Ari put it, "The Step-three microcosm is like the baking powder in a biscuit recipe. There's so little of it used that it seems insignificant, if not completely unnecessary. But you know what happens if you leave the baking powder out? You get something that comes out of the oven looking somewhat like a biscuit, but instead of being light, flaky, fluffy, and delicious, it's flat, hard, chewy, and while slightly edible, it's not at all enjoyable."

Our huddle was like the baking powder in the biscuit—a small thing in an overall recipe for business success, but not one we could skip.

I was relentless. Along with the help of our leadership team, we studied the Habits, took them step-by-step, evaluated our progress often, and kept moving forward. We didn't give up.

I said earlier that we sold NationLink in 2011. To this day, that organization holds a daily huddle at 8:03 every morning. It became that engrained.

Once we saw that Habit begin to take hold, we started on the other Habits: Topgrading, DiSC assessments … everything the book told us to do, we did. It completely changed the way I thought about business. Day by day we moved from frustrated and confused to empowered and enlightened.

YOU MUST WANT CHANGE FOR CHANGE TO OCCUR

That first implementation process taught me a lot, including one very important fact: you must want change for change to occur.

For business owners, this means that one of two conditions must exist: they either need to be so frustrated with their business that they almost don't want to be around their organization anymore, or they're fearful of missing an opportunity.

It's a question we ask all the companies that call us at Petra Coach for our services—"Are you frustrated or scared about where your business is going? Because if you aren't scared, if you aren't frustrated, then you aren't sufficiently inspired. Change won't happen unless you want it."

My inspiration back in 2005 was frustration, and thanks to the Birthing of Giants program at MIT, I realized why: I was a dictator.

I was the person who held all the information, and if anything needed to be done, people had to come to me. I made every decision and answered every question. It was incredibly frustrating, but I didn't want to let it go, because that power gave me security; it gave me a sense of significance in my organization.

It's something I see in entrepreneurs all the time. We'll be in a coaching session and they'll say, "Why the hell does everyone have to come to me?" Then in practically the same breath, they'll say, "I'm not going to let them make their own decisions."

> **WHAT OUR MEMBERS ARE SAYING**
>
> "The dumbest move anyone could make in starting a business is not engaging your team. The simple concept of third-party accountability and having a fresh pair of eyes, not so in the weeds, is invaluable."

You can't have it both ways, and I had to realize that.

GET OUT OF YOUR OWN WAY

Being a dictator got NationLink to a certain point, but it had become a stumbling block—and I kept stumbling on it until my time at the "Birthing of Giants" program taught me that there was another way to do it. That is, I had to get out of my own way.

The Habits gave me and everyone at our organization an operating system to follow, and I had to accept that it was okay to let the team members make their own decisions and do it their way. I had to learn to be okay with a little bit of failure now and then because not everything was going to be the way I wanted it all the time.

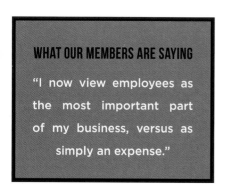

WHAT OUR MEMBERS ARE SAYING

"I now view employees as the most important part of my business, versus as simply an expense."

Over the course of five years or so, I went from being this dictator, asshole leader to a mentor to my team. Prior to that, many of them will tell you that they were afraid of me, but after I learned to accept other people's decisions, to step back and get out of the way, I became more of a confidant—someone they could share information with that they couldn't share with other people. They went from hating being around me to liking to hang out with me, and so I became significant in another and, to me, even more important way.

BECOMING A LION

The idea of being an entrepreneur is glamorous; everyone wants to be a lion. But they only want to be a lion until it's time to do lion shit.

Starting a business, growing a business, hiring and firing, making payroll with a credit card, working past midnight … all of this is the lion shit and it's incredibly difficult, even though a lot of entrepreneurs make it look easy.

But it doesn't have to be that way. You just need to start taking steps, implementing methodologies until they become habits. It certainly doesn't have to be as hard as you're making it or as hard as I made it. In fact, the most difficult part for most business leaders is learning how to set aside that need for control and allowing the strengths of your team members and your faith in their decision-making capabilities to keep the ship sailing powerfully and in the right direction.

At Petra Coach, we've coached entrepreneurs who, at the beginning, couldn't put their phones down or leave for more

> **WHAT OUR MEMBERS ARE SAYING**
>
> "I've had far more time for my children than I would have ever anticipated. It has also freed me up professionally to take our business to the next level by focusing on the strategic big picture, versus being mired in the details."

than a long weekend vacation, and they absolutely couldn't restrain themselves from checking their emails constantly while they were gone.

Eventually, however, they transitioned to not even really needing to go into the office any longer. Now they can go to their kids' soccer games, they can spend their time on strategy, and they can even run another start-up if they want to.

That's what this system does. It provides complete freedom from the things that are tying entrepreneurs down. I did it for myself, and Petra Coach has done it for a lot of other businesses, but only when they're willing to do the work.

It was 4:38 on the afternoon of January 7, 2011, when we sold NationLink for the final time to Resource Communication Group. I stayed on with the organization for a year, but it didn't take long for me to feel disenchanted and completely out of place. Other entrepreneurs have put it this way to me before, and it's true: selling your business and staying on is like watching someone else sleep with your wife … and they really aren't very good at it.

I'd contracted with the new owners to stay on for two years, but at the end of the first year we all agreed it was time for me to move on. My life no longer revolved around NationLink.

It was time to stop wondering where my life was headed and instead design it for myself. ❧

CHAPTER 2: KEY TAKEAWAYS

What's the baking powder in your change biscuit? What's the one little thing your organization does that makes everything else work, much like the baking powder in a biscuit recipe? For us, it was the daily huddle—a small thing in an overall recipe for business success but not one that we could skip.

One of two conditions need to exist for a business to want to implement the Rockefeller Habits: they either have to be frustrated with their business or fearful of missing an opportunity.

For most business leaders, the most difficult part of learning the Habits is learning how to set aside the need for control.

CHAPTER 3

FORMING THE ROCKS: THE CREATION OF PETRA COACH

T he concept of showing others how to implement the Rockefeller Habits[3] had been around for several years. After we got them going at NationLink, other entrepreneurs would reach out to me and ask me about them.

They didn't actually knock on the door and say, "Tell me about the Rockefeller Habits." Instead, they said, "Tell me what you guys are doing—because whatever it is, you're doing it really well. You've got a great culture and we want to know how to do that."

When I told them, "Well, we're doing the Rockefeller Habits," they usually replied with, "What's that and how do I do the same?"

So we began this kind of petri-dish experimental project at NationLink during the last few years I was there. Friends of mine with local companies and, in some cases, even competitors from other states, would come in and spend anywhere from half a day to three full days just observing how we did

---

3   Business operating methodologies rooted in the practices of John D. Rockefeller with pillars of "Priorities," "Data," and "Rhythm" supporting the growth of business.

things. They would go to huddles and attend meetings, and I would give them copies of everything—from how to topgrade to our organization's specific processes and systems. Then, since my last year at NationLink wasn't exactly full-time, I would go to the businesses of some friends and help them get the process going. And they'd pay me a few bucks to do it, too, which was nice.

When I left NationLink, my intention was to keep doing that: helping a few fellow entrepreneurs here and there learn the ins and outs of the Rockefeller Habits methodologies. It wasn't my intent to turn that into a business. I was just going to do that until I could figure out what was next.

The energy I got from helping people grow their businesses and implement the systems and processes of the Rockefeller Habits was incredible. I was

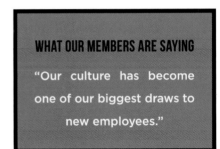

WHAT OUR MEMBERS ARE SAYING

"Our culture has become one of our biggest draws to new employees."

working directly with my tribe—other entrepreneurs who were driven to create something great, and here I was, helping them do it.

When I finally decided to start Petra Coach, our Rockefeller Habits coaching business, I did it just like I tell everyone else to do. I laid out a plan, projecting from my age at the time, forty-five, to age fifty-five. I asked myself what I wanted to accomplish in that ten-year period with the organization, and I began breaking it down, starting with a number of companies to work with (three hundred per year) and working backward to discover what it would take to make it work. I also looked at how I could build the business in a way that was not reliant on my trading time for money, because by this point, I knew myself. I would just keep on trading time for money until I ran out of gas.

My other motivation was maintaining my membership in EO. I'd been a member for fifteen-plus years and was the global membership director at the time I sold NationLink. To do that, and to maintain my ability to serve the EO community at a high level, I had to grow a business—and I had to get it to at least $1 million in revenue in three years or I was out.

Ten years. That put my goal year at 2022, and by that time, I figured we would need twenty coaches with twenty coach team members to serve three hundred member companies going through our process each year.

WHAT OUR MEMBERS ARE SAYING

"Being disciplined with the quarterly meetings and having the entire team involved has made our company stronger."

In 2012 it was just me, and I didn't have a clue as to how I was going to hit that ten-year goal except to do what I already knew—practice what I preached.

From the very first day, I held a daily huddle with myself, recapping the day before and writing down my top priority for the day. I created a one-page strategic plan for Petra Coach and I listed out the quarterly priorities. And since our Align software didn't exist yet, I did this all on paper, clipping it out and sticking it on my wall.

I even created *Core Values*, which have changed very little since they were first created, our *Core Purpose*, and our *Big Hairy Audacious Goal* (BHAG™).

PETRA COACH'S CORE VALUES

- ✓ THERE IS NO TRY!—ONLY DO ...
- ✓ I'VE GOT YOUR BACK, NO MATTER WHAT.
- ✓ "PLEASE" AND "THANK YOU": SAY AND MEAN IT.
- ✓ EVERYTHING IS AN EXPERIENCE, EVERY TIME.
- ✓ SEE AROUND THE CURVES: ANTICIPATE NEEDS AND PRE-FILL THEM.
- ✓ BE CURIOUS: ASK "WHY" AND IMPROVE.

PETRA COACH'S CORE PURPOSE

Our purpose, or 'why we exist' is deeply rooting in our own history of clearly understanding that we, as human beings, must continually change in order to achieve what we want to achieve. The primary question is 'WHO' do we need to become in order to achieve what we what to achieve. Leading us to our Core Purpose of Changing Live 3 Layers Deep - The head, The heart, The soul and is restated as Have a positive impact on 10,000,000 human beings or +10Mhb.

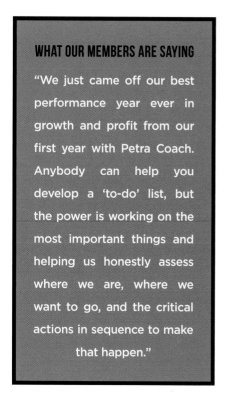

WHAT OUR MEMBERS ARE SAYING

"We just came off our best performance year ever in growth and profit from our first year with Petra Coach. Anybody can help you develop a 'to-do' list, but the power is working on the most important things and helping us honestly assess where we are, where we want to go, and the critical actions in sequence to make that happen."

PETRA COACH'S BIG HAIRY AUDACIOUS GOAL

Finally, there was the BHAG. With the long term vision of having a 'place' where leaders and learners gather to grow together we set our north star as The Petra Playground envisioning a 'playground' or campus where the future leaders of business could come together, learn and go then grow others.

WHAT "PETRA" MEANS— THE STORY OF NAMING PETRA

We didn't start off with the name "Petra." We were called "Rock Habits" and that name is still on our LLC. But after talking with Verne Harnish, we decided that the name was too close to "Rockefeller Habits," so we started brainstorming on a new one.

We had a few more people who did project work with us in trade for coaching by this point, and I remember grabbing three of them—Ben Rigsby and Mark Scrivner, who did excellent videography for us, and our PR guy, Jeff Bradford—and locking us all up in a conference room with the sole purpose of figuring out a new name for our coaching organization based around Rockefeller Habits.

I can still see them sitting there, Ben and Mark with their Macs open and Jeff with the biggest damn dictionary you've ever seen, throwing phrases and names around and finding one reason or another to scrap each one.

After two or three hours of this, we had a wall of sticky notes with names on it, but none of them felt *right*. Then it hit me—a friend of mine with a staffing organization called Vaco once told me that the reason he chose his organization's name was because it was Latin for "free yourself."

"Why don't we look at Latin?" I said.

Jeff thought about it for a second and then said, "Your organization isn't timid, right? You need a name that blows air out when you say it, that's forceful..." He dug around in a reference book for a few minutes and then said, "What about the Latin word for 'rock,' petra?"

That was it. We talked about the story of the city of Petra, which is this incredible community carved from solid stone in the Kingdom of Jordan some two thousand years ago and how our goal was to help others be legendary and last for years. It was right, it fit: from that day, we were Petra Coach.

THANK GOODNESS FOR INTERNS

Even though I had successfully built and exited NationLink, it had been eighteen years since I went through the start-up process and I'd forgotten a ton.

The little things that I'd forgotten suddenly became nagging tasks that threw off the whole day. I had to do my own billing again, putting stamps on envelopes and sending them myself—whereas we used to have a department that did all that. Even simple things like throwing out the trash became a time suck, because it was just me doing all of it, and that $1 million in revenue qualification for EO membership seemed more and more difficult to reach.

Thank goodness for interns. Right around the time I was realizing how in over my head I was as a one-man start-up, a student from the local high school gave me a call.

"Mr. Bailey," she said, "my name is Katie Schimmel at Franklin Road Academy. We're starting an internship program and we're looking for local companies that would like to participate. Would you be interested?"

Here I am drowning in things I can't do myself and here's this girl, all of fifteen or sixteen years old, asking if I could use some free help. Of course I was interested, I told her. I didn't know what I'd need her to do off the top of my head, apart from mailing letters and keeping the office neat, but I'd love to talk with her about it.

A few days later, she came to the office with her teacher and after we went over the nature of Petra Coach and what I would need, she asked if she could have the job.

Katie was by far the sharpest high school kid I'd ever met. Since the time she started working with me I've had other interns—college and even post-graduate students who worked with us part-time or during the summer—and I would put her against any one of them, even though she was just a junior in high school.

Even at that age she had an incredibly strong entrepreneurial and financially oriented mind-set. She took on all those little tasks that were driving me nuts and allowed me to focus on the things I needed to do to really get the company in motion. She saw gaps, and when she found one, she asked me if she could fix it for me.

It was Katie, in fact, who created the first Petra Coach *playbook*, which is a cornerstone of our implementation process to this day. She went to planning sessions and suggested documents to help with processes that made total sense but I'd not given the time before.

For two years, she helped me get Petra Coach off the ground until finally I was able to bring on the first full-time team member. And I knew exactly who I needed to call: Mandy!

MANDY JOINS THE TEAM

For as long as I can remember, I've kept an Evernote list of people I've met whom I would call "A-Players." It could be someone I bumped into at a restaurant, through an organization, or in a social setting who impressed me in a certain way and could be the kind of team player I'd need on a team one day.

The list has close to seventy-five people on it and spans all areas of life, and at the very top of that list was Mandy Burage.

Mandy worked with me at NationLink for close to seven years and stayed with NationLink after we sold it. When it came to decision making, she unfailingly chose what was in the best interest of the organization and our members, not her own. She had an incredible work ethic and we worked well together. I could trust her.

Several months after I left NationLink she called to talk about how things were going, and overall I got the impression that she wasn't happy there. I couldn't offer her a job at the time, but I remembered that call when I was finally able to bring someone on.

I wanted to reach out to her directly to tell her about the position, but I had a non-solicitation agreement as part of the sale, so I tried a couple of peripheral approaches, posting on LinkedIn and Facebook in the hopes she might see it and get in touch, but she never did.

The funny thing was, our offices were in the same building, yet I couldn't figure out a way to speak with her about the job without violating my agreement.

Finally, I just walked over to the NationLink offices to speak to the CEO and said, "Look, I get the feeling Mandy's not happy where she is and I'd like the opportunity to talk with her about working with my organization. But we have a non-solicitation, so I can't do that without your permission. So would you rather lose her to the world when she finally up and quits, or would you rather have her down the hall where you could ask her a question if you needed to?"

Fortunately, the CEO said I could talk with her, and Mandy agreed to come on.

Mandy couldn't have come on board soon enough.

The demand for coaching was getting to the point where there just weren't enough days in the calendar to fit everyone in, and we were having to turn companies away simply because we couldn't book them quickly enough (often as much as six months out).

It was time to start bringing on new coaches, which presented a whole new type of challenge. Via coaching, I'd helped dozens of companies scale up, creating systems and processes that could be followed by anyone. But how do you find people who can coach others through those processes and do it well?

Mandy and I had to sit down and map out the profile of what our ideal coach looked like: his or her attributes, background, personality … all those things that are integral to someone we knew we could work well with, who would do the job well, and most importantly, someone we could trust. And one attribute we discovered early on was that the best coaches—the very best—were entrepreneurial themselves. ❧

THE EARLY DAYS OF PETRA COACH

KATIE'S VIEW

My internship at Petra Coach was only supposed to be one week long—a spring semester project in 2012 for our business class. But I was really interested in business and Andy and I just hit it off during the interview.

Two years later, I finally had to leave Petra Coach to start college. In those two years, though, I learned a lot about the fundamentals of business, planning, and strategic management that not only helped me in my college classes but in my personal life, as well.

The first Petra Coach office was in the old NationLink building in a space that might have once been used for storage. It was really, really small, but it felt cozy and we had everything we needed. There was Andy's desk, a TV, a couple of whiteboards, a mini-fridge, and this giant printer.

I remember we killed a lot of trees in those early days, printing off tons of paper for meetings. We didn't have the Align software—Petra Coach's business-management platform—back then, so our materials were either printed out or, if we needed something larger like posters, I'd write them out by hand. I also took care of the social-media aspect, connecting Petra with platforms like Facebook and Twitter and put together our first Petra Coach Playbooks.

What made it easy, and what really impressed me about Andy, was that he was always on his A-game. If he was out of town, he'd always leave me instructions on what needed to be done that day, whether it was client bags that needed to be packed up (those little gift bags with things like candy and Yoda bobbleheads) or paperwork that he needed prepared.

It was incredibly organized, and I always knew exactly which client I was preparing for.

The importance of having that organizational mind-set was a valuable lesson for me. At the same time, putting together those client packets, each of them completely personalized to each organization, taught me the value of being personable and making sure you appreciate who you work with and who works with you.

Working at Petra Coach changed everything for me. It gave me confidence, because I had this really cool job that nobody else in my high school had—and Andy treated me like a full-time team member. He even bought me a new laptop to replace the old one I had from high school, and I loved it because I felt like I'd worked really hard to earn it.

I'm so grateful to have been able to work at Petra Coach. Andy's a great coach and a great person to work with, and I would not be where I am today—working as an accountant and studying for a master of accountancy degree—if not for him. He taught me more about building a business than I ever could have learned in a classroom setting.

—*Katie Schimmel*

PETRA COACH'S FIRST ACCOUNTABILITY COACH

MANDY'S VIEW

I continued to run my department at NationLink after Andy sold the organization, but after he left, the culture changed and the atmosphere was just different.

I couldn't wait to get back to the culture I'd grown to love so much, so when Andy offered me a position with Petra Coach, I was thrilled ... even though I wasn't entirely sure what he meant at first when he said he was coaching the process from a book we'd read eight years ago.

I had a ton of questions, but Andy walked me through the whole thing—what Gazelles was, how he was a certified coach, and how he was now teaching the process to other businesses the same way he'd implemented the Rockefeller Habits at NationLink so many years ago.

It took him a while to explain it because my impression of the Rockefeller Habits was that you couldn't just learn them and "turn them on." It had taken us years to implement them and really get them right. But that was all part of the process, he said. All I knew of the Habits was the outcome. What companies needed to be *coached* on was how to actively implement the process.

It's funny because today the coaching process is so ingrained in what I do, but I still see that same question mark in new hires that lit across my face when Andy explained what Petra Coach was to me for the first time.

"So we're teaching a book?" they ask me.

"Yes."

"Then couldn't people just go out and buy the book and teach themselves?" they ask.

"You know, that's the same question I had when I started," I say. "And they could. Some do! But the process is infinitely easier when you have someone who knows the methodologies backward and forward to guide you through it and hold you accountable."

It's a little difficult to explain, but once you get it, you really get it.

On my second day of working with Petra Coach, for instance, I went to my first planning session with Andy.

He asked me to come and take notes, talk to the organization, and share my experiences in implementing the Habits at NationLink. Again, this was my **second day** there and he was standing in front of this room full of high-powered CEOs saying, "Mandy, go ahead and share a struggle you had at NationLink when you were implementing this."

Andy is the king of getting you out of your comfort zone. But it got me to deal with my nervousness of speaking in front of crowds and gave me the strength to share my stories with others.

In fact, a story that I share a lot these days is about my time on maternity leave. I was out for three months with our new baby girl and during that time I felt like I was working harder than I'd ever worked in my entire life, and yet there was zero appreciation. My husband did what he could, of course, but he was still learning how to be a dad and clearly my baby couldn't appreciate me, so there was no one else. It just felt like this really thankless job.

But when I came back to work after three months, I was greeted with piles of notes on my desk, tons of welcomes, people telling me how much they missed me, and just this level of appreciation that I'd missed so much and never realized it until then.

I shared this story for the first time at a two-day kickoff with a new member company, and the next day, one of the clients came up to me and said, "Hey, I just wanted to let you know how thankful I am that you shared that story about your maternity leave and the importance of feeling appreciated. My wife is home right now with our four-week-old daughter and last night I wrote her a thank-you note and brought her flowers. She broke down in tears, because she thought no one was noticing. So thank you for sharing that story."

I couldn't believe how powerful that was, to have that person tell me how much of an impact I'd made in his life just by sharing my story.

That's what we do, as coaches and accountability coaches. We change lives. It's an amazing process to participate in, to see the state an organization is in when it starts and then work with them—teach them best practices, guide them, give them suggestions, and then see them implement them and improve across the board. It's incredibly rewarding.

My role at Petra Coach has changed a lot over time, from sitting in the corner taking notes to managing the coach-coordinator team, supporting the coaches, and at the end of the day, making sure that the clients implement the Rockefeller Habits and keep them moving along in the process.

It's a lot of work, and the expectations in our organization are high, but I love that because it means that I can expect really great things from my team. And we can never say that our leader isn't being fair—because Andy will outwork any person I've ever met, ten to one.

There's a lot of trust, a lot of respect at Petra Coach—and a lot of learning as well. Every time I feel like I'm getting comfortable, Andy will push me out of it and drive me to continue learning.

When I started with Petra Coach, I truly did not see myself doing anything like this, but now I can't imagine doing anything else.

—Mandy Burage, Director of Operations
and Accountability Coach

CHAPTER 3: KEY TAKEAWAYS

I started Petra Coach the same way I tell others to start their businesses: I laid out a plan, asked myself where I wanted to be in ten years, and worked backward to discover what it would take to make that work.

"Petra" is Latin for "rock" and symbolizes our goal to help other companies build on a rock-solid foundation.

Petra coaches and accountability coaches change lives. They work with companies to teach them best practices, guide them as they implement the Habits, and improve across the board.

In determining whom we needed to bring on as Petra Coaches, we realized that the very best coaches were entrepreneurial themselves.

CHAPTER 4

SCALING THE UNSCALABLE

The urge to trade time for money was a trap I fell into early on in my career. It was something I did with sales and something I started doing with the coaching business to work out the kinks and build a scalable process.

Coaches don't have a lot of product. We don't have a lot of ancillary services that people subscribe to, so we trade our expertise, information, and insights for income.

But there's only so much salable time in one person's day, and I knew that to grow, we needed to produce *more* time—and that meant scaling up and bringing on more coaches.

But how do you take something that's traditionally one-person coaching and turn it into a coaching organization?

I thought about it for a while and finally decided to go see Keith Cupp, who at the time was the CEO of Gazelles International.

Gazelles International was the coaching association for *Scaling Up*, the most recent iteration of Verne Harnish's *Mastering the Rockefeller Habits*, and my question for Keith was, "Who in Gazelles has a coaching organization rather than just working as an individual coach?"

Keith explained that there were a few people attempting to build a coaching organization and pushing hard on it and a few others that had tried and decided to stop—but no one was doing it at the level I knew I could take it to.

The idea of creating a coaching organization *inside* a coaching organization was uncharted territory, but all that meant was that the mistakes were there for me to make.

If I was going to scale to $1 million annually and hit my ten-year, three-hundred-member goal, I knew I'd need to have twenty coaches with twenty team members by 2022. In 2012, however, I was the only coach and I needed a plan to get there.

When Mandy finally started in her full-time role at Petra Coach, looking for coaches became one of our top priorities. We knew we needed to create coaching systems and processes that were repeatable so that anyone with a skill set could follow them and do the job; but doing it and doing it *well* are two different things.

We needed to find *entrepreneurs*—people who have owned or operated a business in some form or fashion. They didn't necessarily have to be owners, but they needed to be heavily involved in the operation. Simply put, we needed people with skin in the game.

SKIN IN THE GAME

It's one thing to find entrepreneurs and it's another to find ones with all the qualities that make a good coach.

Good coaches have to be able to get in front of a room and make people listen. They need to garner respect and speak the truth, even if the truth isn't something that the people in the room want to hear. They need to make people want to perform, to put in the hard work to make the coach proud of them.

I've heard so many gasps in meetings that I can't even count them anymore, and every time I hear one, I wonder if they're either going to kick me out or just kick me. But I say the truth, because it feels like the right thing to do.

It takes the right kind of knowledge and experience—and enough guts to bring it all into the danger zone—even if it's not what people want to hear. *That's* what makes a great coach … that and about fifty other things.

TAKING THE RISK

Our coaches[4] at Petra Coach are all entrepreneurial, so we give them lots of space to create the best approach with each organization. We guide them on the process of implementation—and they go do it. It's no different than how we coach our clients: "This is the process; now it's up to you to perform."

Training includes Petra Academy, Petra University sessions, attending and participating in planning sessions, and being able to lead a session independently with only an observing coach in the room by the last session.

Additionally, each coach is required to complete the Gazelles Certification process, which includes online training, book assignments, live training, mentoring with a senior coach and an accountability coach, planing session presentations and attendance at Scaleup Summits.

Above all, however, are the *Core Values*:

---

4   Learn more about each of our coaches at www.PetraCoach.com/meet-the-coaches.

- ✓ THERE IS NO TRY!—ONLY DO ...

- ✓ I'VE GOT YOUR BACK, NO MATTER WHAT.

- ✓ "PLEASE" AND "THANK YOU": SAY AND MEAN IT.

- ✓ EVERYTHING IS AN EXPERIENCE, EVERY TIME.

- ✓ SEE AROUND THE CURVES: ANTICIPATE NEEDS AND PRE-FILL THEM.

- ✓ BE CURIOUS: ASK "WHY" AND IMPROVE.

Agree to all of these, live by them, and you're on your way to being a Petra Coach. Of course, that still doesn't mean you'll make it—but not everyone who tries out for the NBA ends up getting signed, either.

COACHES AGREEMENT

The very first line of Petra Coach's Coaches Agreement, which every coach agrees to, is taken from a quote that Tom Landry often used to describe what it means to be a coach: "A Petra Coach is someone who *tells you what you don't want to hear* and who has you *see what you don't want to see*, so that you can *become what you have always known you could be!*"

It's not an agreement to be taken lightly. IIt requires that every coach live by the high standards of Petra and Gazelles, and position him or herself as the one that Petra Coach members naturally look to for leadership, advice, direction, and insight.

Becoming a Petra Coach is rare. You do not apply for it—you're selected. After that, it's up to the prospective coach to own the process and fight for it.

ACCOUNTABILITY COACHES

> **WHAT OUR MEMBERS ARE SAYING**
>
> "The Petra team brings thousands of hours of implementing the Rockefeller Habits and pours that knowledge into our team. This allows us to avoid many of the pitfalls and mistakes that have inhibited others and drives our culture of accountability and personal growth. It has been one of the most rewarding ways for us to invest in our team both professionally and personally."

Just as valuable to the Petra Coach team as good coaches are our accountability coaches. If the coaches are the face of Petra Coach, then the accountability coaches are its heart and lungs.

The coaches' number-one priority is the member, and the accountability coaches make that possible. When a coach sets up a planning session, for instance, the accountability coaches take care of everything, from logistics to travel to agendas to shipping materials. They book the venue, manage the day-of process, send out reminder emails, update one-page plans. They handle recapping, invoicing, collections, payment processing … all of it. That way the coaches have little else to focus on apart from delivering their maximum energy to the coaching process, which is a marathon in and of itself.

In the times between planning sessions, the accountability coaches also manage specific check-ins with members, making sure that team members who have been assigned a responsibility as part of the Rockefeller Habits are implementing them.

And just like the coaches, the accountability coaches also attend their own versions of training. Once he or she is ready, an accountability coaches has done just as many planning sessions as a coach, if not more, and has a complete understanding of the implementation process.

I believe in the law of attraction, that if we put something in our minds in a very clear fashion, that things will happen for us and allow us to achieve it. I had that belief when I began looking for good coaches and accountability coaches, and I still had it when I first came across the challenge of reducing the complexity of literally hundreds of documents generated for one client as part of the Petra process.

Fortunately, one of our very first members was just the guy to help us win that paper challenge.

CREATING *ALIGN*

When I originally implemented the Rockefeller Habits—inside NationLink—it was all on paper. We would print these large-format copies of the one-page plan and put them up on the wall, print posters of the priorities, and just use up a lot of paper in general.

That was all I knew at first, the paper side of it. We'd store sheets in places like Dropbox or Excel, of course, but when it came down to it, those were all still pieces of paper—they didn't interact, they simply existed.

If it hadn't been for an organization called Aptify and its founder, Amith Nagarajan, Petra Coach would likely still be on paper and not even close to our BHAG of impacting ten million human beings.

I'd met Amith back in 2010 at an Entrepreneurs' Organization (EO) meeting in Nashville, and later he became one of our very first members.

Even back then, Aptify—which is a developer of application software for enterprise-class associations, nonprofits, and other member-based organizations—already had international offices, with a strong research and development team in India.

Because of this, part of our engagement involved going to India and coaching the team there, bringing them up to speed on the process, and implementing a few of the methodologies that the Aptify teams in the States were already doing.

It was a rewarding week, and on the twelve-hour flight home, Amith and I chatted about the next steps in the process. We were just getting into the priorities-tracking process when he turned to me and said, "Andy, this methodology is great. The whole idea of alignment and the culture and everything else we're doing is awesome. Everybody is excited about it, but there's one problem—how do I know for sure how well-aligned my team is relative to the organization's goals for the quarter or year or for any time period?"

WHAT OUR MEMBERS ARE SAYING

"I've been able to do more of the big-picture items now that our team has clear objectives and I can track their progress in Align."

I thought about it for a second and said, "Dude, there are two hundred pieces of paper in the Dropbox folder we can pull and walk through, but it's so complex. We can put it into an Excel spreadsheet, even do some pivot tables and figure it out …"

Amith stopped me right there.

"Andy, look, I'm a software guy and you're in the coaching business. Let's team up and build a new application that would be easy for people to use and would solve all of these problems."

We spent the next few hours on the plane talking through what a dashboard for Petra Coach might look like.

At first, it was literally just a dashboard with priorities on it that allowed users to enter their own priorities and then see those of everyone else in their organization. In fact, Amith and his team originally tried to find an existing online tool or web app that could function as a basic structure for managing everything we needed it to manage on a global basis—but after they dug into it a little, they realized there was really no good solution out there.

It would have to be built as a new application, which is a pretty big undertaking, but it turned out that Amith had just spun out a new custom-software-development company called Radolo that could do everything we needed.

Radolo not only created software but they also had this rapid application-development process that was perfect for what we needed. It started any new software platform with a code base that was partially complete, leaving only seventy percent left to customize—a balance that allowed for plenty of creativity while cutting out the labor-intensive process of building a unique foundation.

> **WHAT OUR MEMBERS ARE SAYING**
>
> "We've always had great people, but having the transparency of Align has allowed me to clearly see their growth, the priorities they take on, and how passionate they are about improving a certain aspect of the company."

Align was Radolo's first project.

Their team, under the leadership of developer Josh Grippo, used the rapid application-development platform, and about six months later we had our first version of Align.

It took another year to really smooth things out, and even today we're constantly improving on it, but in that relatively brief period of time, Align quickly became the number-one software tool in the Rockefeller Habits space.

Oddly enough, when we started working on the new software we had no idea that there was such a huge need for something like this in the coaching community or even the business community at large.

Today we offer the Align software through Gazelles coaches for companies implementing the Rockefeller Habits, but close to 40 percent of Align users are small-to-medium businesses who aren't practicing the Rockefeller Habits but are still using it to track things like daily huddles and priorities. All told, as of 2017 we'd reached more than eight thousand users in sixty-four countries who, combined, had completed more than 250,000 priorities.

When we started building Align, we never could have dreamed it would become what it is today. That first platform had a ton of bugs and issues, but you have to start somewhere. Now we're at the stage where it's really growing—doubling in size every twelve months—which tells me that once we put some fuel on that fire, it can be ten times what it is today. And of course that's what we're doing. ❧

CHAPTER 4: KEY TAKEAWAYS

Good coaches need to be able to make people listen. They need to garner respect and speak the truth, even if it's not something people want to hear.

Accountability coaches allow coaches to make their member companies their number-one priority.

The Align software—Petra Coach's proprietary software for tracking organizational priorities in real-time—was created with the help of one of its first clients: Amith Nagarajan of Aptify. It was created as a way to avoid having to shuffle through the hundreds of documents created throughout the planning process.

The Align software is now offered through Gazelles coaches, as well as to small-to-medium businesses in general. As of 2017, Align had more than eight thousand users in sixty-four countries who, combined, have achieved more than half a million priorities.

CHAPTER 5

THE PETRA COACH EXPERIENCE

"If we're growing, we're always going
to be out of our comfort zone."

JOHN MAXWELL

"If you really want to be here today, you're a little weird."

I've said this in front of any number of companies as we kicked off their first quarterly planning session, and it's true, even for our own organization. When you're beginning the Rockefeller Habits in your business, it's not easy taking an entire day, possibly more, away from that massive pile of work, the ringing phones, and the demanding customers, to spend time thinking about what's working, what's not working, what's next, where you're going, and how you get there.

But it's necessary. And if you're going to make the Habits work for you—really work for you—then you have to treat them as ritual. You have to reset your mind so that these methods aren't something you *should* do but are rather something you *have* to do. You have to tell yourself, "Dammit, I'm going to do this, because I don't want my organization to be where it was. Something has to change and *this is part of that change.*"

THE ENGAGEMENT PERIOD

We don't take on just any organization at Petra Coach. We'll get calls or emails or texts or even Facebook messages from businesses all over the world asking about our coaching services, and the first person they speak with is one of our qualifiers. We have to understand what their true need is first and whether or not there'll be a mutually good fit before moving forward.

> **WHAT OUR MEMBERS ARE SAYING**
>
> "Having an outside perspective is critical to the growth of our company. We take our planning more seriously knowing we have a meeting rhythm. Petra helps us get rid of squishy goals, have tough conversations, and think differently to reach big goals."

During that initial call with a candidate, we ask a series of behavioral questions and listen for a few things that help us determine if they are:

1. **PERSONAL GROWTH-ORIENTED VS. GOAL-ORIENTED**

    Is the organization really interested in being better or are they just interested in accomplishing goals? Personal growth-oriented companies are automatically goal-oriented but not the other way around. Leadership has to be personally committed to changing itself before others if the methodologies are going to work.

2. **WILLING TO REPRODUCE THEMSELVES**

   A business has to be willing to let go of things in order to grow. Leadership has to be willing to reproduce itself, to share information so others can take on responsibilities. People don't get better automatically—you have to invest in them.

3. **ABLE TO COMMIT TO APPLICATION**

   Leaders must be willing to take what they learn and apply it *immediately* to themselves. They must be willing to take the things we tell them to do on faith—and just go do them until they believe in them and it all becomes a part of their culture; a habit.

4. **IN THE RIGHT MIND-SET**

   They have to be in at least one of the two emotional states that are conducive to change: either so *frustrated* with their business that they're willing to do anything to change it, or *fearful* of missing an opportunity, because they have no way of achieving it if they keep doing what they're currently doing.

Of course, we ask the typical questions, too, like number of team members, revenue, margin, what books they read—all in an effort to ensure the best fit. And we ask about complexity, too, such as whether they're in multiple locations, if they're family-owned, if there are multiple heads-of-business, and other factors that may make it more costly to conduct the coaching process properly. But what helps us discern a *good fit* is how well a candidate fits into those four behavioral requirements.

Sandbox ❓

12 - 36 Month \ $5M-$100M \ 15 - 500 \ North America - Europe

DOMINATE the delivery of 12-36 month implementation programs for $5 - $50M firms in North America.

- 15-500 team member businesses.
- $5M-$100M top line revenue businesses.
- Entrepreneurial owner operated businesses.
- Lifetime learner leadership teams.
- Financially viable to pay for services.

Ideal Client Profile (*interview for these attributes*)

1. Personal Growth Oriented VS. Goal Oriented - if leadership is growth oriented they will automatically be goal oriented. At a minimum they must we willing to become growth oriented. Personally committed to change themselves before others.
2. Reproduce Themselves - a business cannot be great unless it can be great beyond just leadership. They must be willing to take the information and share it and truly want to grow others. People don't get automatically better, it's an investment.
3. Commit to Application - leadership must take the information and apply it *immediately* themselves, it cannot be a coaches place to ensure application.
4. Financially Viable to Pay for Services - do they have the financial ability to pay for our services without it causing issues with the business.

Conditions that exist... possibly in combination

- Frustrated with business - leadership is so frustrated and unhappy that they will do anything to change it, they have hit a wall of some sort and cannot get past it.
- Fear of missing an opportunity - leadership can see an opportunity but realizes that there is no way they can achieve it doing what they are doing today.
  ○ *"If everything is good - OK - not too difficult - change will not occur (at least easily)*

Petra Coach's Sandbox in the One-Page Strategic Plan in Align

What we *don't* want to happen is to discover, several months later, that the coach cares more about the business than the business does—and that has happened a surprising number of times. It makes no sense to put all this time and effort into teaching an organization how to improve if they're not going to put those teachings into practice. The results are commensurate with the effort, and if the leaders of an organization are just using their business as a bank account, then there's no point in continuing our relationship.

So we do our best to weed out these types of businesses early and look for the ones that are really willing to go all in, in order to change.

THE COACH MATCH

When a candidate makes it through the initial vetting process, we have an internal conversation to determine which coach would be best for them, based on factors such as industry knowledge, history, availability, geographic location, and personality type.

WHAT OUR MEMBERS ARE SAYING

"After engaging with Petra, you will wonder how your business survived before."

After that, there's an additional call among the candidate, accountability coach, and the candidate's ideal coach that goes deeper than any of the earlier calls. This explains the implementation process, what to expect, which dates to begin, investment, and finally, verbally verifying an agreement that is then sent to them for approval. At that point, we've gained a new member and the coaching process kicks off.

THE PAPERWORK

It's usually about a four-week period between the day a new member says "Go!" with us and the first session, during which time we do a whole list of things—most of it is gathering information so we can get the most accurate picture possible of where the organization is, financially and organizationally. We also get the initial setup of the Align tool, loading their data and creating the organization's rough one-page plan from the data provided.

At the same time, we're collecting hard materials like past strategic planning documents and org charts. We're also collecting data on the intangibles, such as conducting a survey to get a feel for what's going on in the organization on an inter-relational level.

A lot of conversations happen before that first planning session. The coach will hold calls with leadership, talking through the process and what to expect during that first meeting, including who's going to be in the room in each session.

The point of all this discovery is to understand the business from all sides—to get a lay of the land and formulate as accurate a game plan as possible for that first session. We don't want to be up-to-speed with the

> **WHAT OUR MEMBERS ARE SAYING**
>
> "Best decision we've ever made in our business. It's not an insignificant investment but well worth the money."

state of the organization by that first planning session—we want to be up-to-speed well *before* we get there so we can have everything in place and ready to go on day one.

THE KICK-OFF—DAY ONE

When it comes to planning sessions, we start small and build participation as we go, beginning with the executive leadership team, because we need leadership's buy-in first. They need to be doing the huddles first, getting into the meeting rhythms first, doing the work before they ask anyone else to do the work.

But the first question—the very first question we ask—is "why?" Why do they want to implement this process?

We don't accept the standard, marketing-approved soundbite answer to this question, either. We don't want them to say, "So we'll be better as an organization" or "So we can make more money" or "So we can get that contract with *x*."

What we want them to say is, "Because all through college I never lost a football game. I never failed in my life. I'm failing today and I'm sick of it," or "My dad was a successful entrepreneur, made millions of dollars, and sold three businesses, and I haven't been able to do that yet. He doesn't think I can do it and I'm going to prove him wrong."

Right off the bat, we push them out of their comfort zone and get them to clearly understand why they're ready for change. Then we use that answer—their real "why"—for the rest of their engagement. Every time someone doesn't show up for a call or cuts corners like the daily huddle, we bring that message right back to them and reestablish the deep, emotional connection for why they want—why they need—change.

It's not an easy process. There's usually a bunch of nervousness and even some tears. I've had guys look me in the eye as if they were going to punch me, but I just kept on them until that personal connection was made.

Some things we'll accomplish on that first day and some things we won't, but the goal is to get the executive leadership team to complete as much of the following as possible on day one.

WHAT OUR MEMBERS ARE SAYING

"After six months in 'the program,' I am seeing more forward movement with my team. And there seems to be less stress and more teamwork given the improved communication via daily huddles, weekly strategy meetings, and two-weekers."

WHY DO YOU EXIST?

Once we answer the "Why do you want to do this?" question, we move on to the next question: "What is the purpose of this organization? Why do you exist?"

This is where we discover the core purpose of the organization, creating an initial draft that they can let sit and bake with the organization for a period of time to make sure they're right and tweak it if need be.

After we have our core purpose, we move to our core values—one of the most used and, in my opinion, most important areas to get right. Core values, as stated by Verne Harnish in *Scaling Up*, are the handful of rules defining an organization's culture, which are reinforced by people-management systems on a daily basis. These are the "behaviors" most valued in a business—the short list of non-negotiables that everyone must live by. Setting a solid group of core values becomes a cornerstone for many areas of business improvement and should not be taken lightly. During day one, we work to get our original draft of core values set for the organization.

We also work on the organization's Big Hairy Audacious Goal—what they ultimately want their business to achieve—because a lot of the time, they've never even thought about it—and if they have, they're probably not thinking nearly large enough.

We want to build a long-term picture of the organization, picking a date in the future that we can reasonably shoot for and creating a plan to get there. Rapidly growing businesses, for instance, may have a three-year timeframe while a long-established business, say one that's been making bricks for 115 years, may be comfortable with a five-year timeframe.

Whatever the timeframe, we pick a date and say, "On this day, this is where we want to be," and then we break everything down into two segments: targets and key thrusts.

Targets are that line in the sand that says, "Come hell or high water, this is where we're going." They're the hard metrics, things like revenue, gross margin, profits, new locations, and number of contracts over one million dollars, among other things.

What's interesting, however, and what I've seen a lot of companies do, is look at that theoretical date and then go backward.

"If our average growth rate over the last five years was x," they'll say, "and we did y last year, then z is where we'll be in three or five years."

To me, none of that matters much. It's important information, but for this discussion, it doesn't matter. The question isn't "Where do you *estimate* you'll be?"—it's "Where do you *want* to be?" And once we figure that out, we talk about how we're going to get there. If, in the discussion, we determine that it's too expensive, too difficult, or you have to rob a bank to fund it, then we can adjust the target. But if you start from, "We've been at 15 percent for a year so we can probably be at 15 percent a year from now," you're never going to achieve your maximum result.

Forget the past. Put a stake in the ground, say you're going from $10 million annually to $50 million in three years, and determine what targets you'll need to hit to get there, what key thrusts you'll need to build to reach those targets, and what strengths, weaknesses, opportunities, and threats (SWOT) need to be prioritized to get there.

Does that forward-geared planning work? Hell yeah, it does. Chapters 6 through 12 showcase how companies of all sizes pulled off the impossible by just answering, "Where do you want to be?"

With those hard targets in mind, we can then look at how the organization is going to reach those targets—what they're capable of. Those capabilities are their key thrusts—things they have to do really well in order to reach those targets. In pinpointing the thrusts needed to reach a set of targets, we create a vision of an end result that gives us the ability to create shorter-term initiatives and priorities to make it come true.

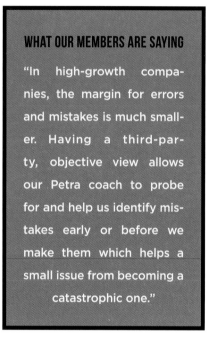

WHAT OUR MEMBERS ARE SAYING

"In high-growth companies, the margin for errors and mistakes is much smaller. Having a third-party, objective view allows our Petra coach to probe for and help us identify mistakes early or before we make them which helps a small issue from becoming a catastrophic one."

If, for instance, we determine that an organization has a three-year target of fifty-two new contracts of $1 million or more, then we need to make sure they have the capability of a *repeatable, scalable sales process and a team of people to support it.* If they only have three people on the sales team right now, and each salesperson has a different process, then one approach might be to have *fifty salespeople all using the same system with the highest return rate.* This fully stocked, highly efficient team would then be the thrust the organization needs to hit that three-year target.

SWOT—STRENGTHS, WEAKNESSES, OPPORTUNITIES, AND THREATS

A lot of people do SWOT and then stick it in a drawer and never use it because they don't know—or they don't take the time—to figure out how to put it to work.

With the Petra Coach process, however, SWOT is dynamic: we have a set of strengths and we look for potential priorities every quarter to protect them. We have a set of weaknesses and we look for potential priorities in the quarter that can help

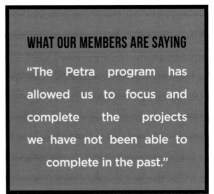

WHAT OUR MEMBERS ARE SAYING

"The Petra program has allowed us to focus and complete the projects we have not been able to complete in the past."

eliminate them. Opportunities—those things we want to achieve long-term—need to be prioritized and records kept of how we're closing in on taking advantage of them. The same thing goes for threats, with a possible priority chosen each quarter for mitigating one or more.

Every other quarter, we'll look at the organization's SWOT and ask, "Is this still a strength or is something else more of a strength today? Is this still an opportunity or has another one taken its place?"

SWOT becomes a living document that leadership can use to make good decisions for a dynamically growing organization.

Then we'll build out the year by saying, "If example x needs to be true in three years, what has to be true this year? Where are we going this year?"

This kind of approach helps organizations avoid the two barriers that often hold a business back from growing the way it should: people and processes. For a company to grow, it needs to bring on more qualified people, and it needs to have the processes in place to handle the complexities that come with that growth. By planning ahead and looking at how many people you'll need to hire, how they'll be able to communicate most effectively, and how decisions will be made in that growing environment, you can proactively steer that growth away from becoming a weakness and toward the category it should fall in: a solid strength.

THE FIRST PLANNING SESSION— DAY TWO OF THE KICK-OFF

On the second day, more of the team joins in, from management or supervisors to, in some cases, the entire organization.

To kick off the session, we recap the work we completed on day one for the team members who are joining for the first time, painting the picture of what the organization will look like in three or five years so they are clear and can discuss it with others.

One of the greatest things I've learned, and that I've seen others come to realize, is that a business must engage the entire team to maximize results. Exposing the broader team to planning does two very important things:

1. It gives them the thirty-thousand-foot view of the business, beyond just what they do each day. This is a light bulb moment for them. They finally understand how they fit into the bigger puzzle.

2. Because they are involved in the process of creating the priorities, they have ownership in them far beyond any level that's merely dictated to them.

It's also an opportunity to talk about the executive leadership's draft of the core purpose, core values, and BHAG, and ask the team what they think of and feel about them—all the while painting this big vision of where the organization is going in the foreseeable future.

The crux of this second day, however, is not so much in reviewing the goals we set in day one but in accomplishing them. As a group, we begin to define each person's three to five priorities for the quarter and the tasks that need to be achieved in that time to reach the organization's one-quarter, one-year, and three-to-five-year outcomes. Then we enter that information directly into our Align software. So everything is set for execution at the end of the day.

Ninety days later, we meet again for our second quarterly planning session and review how the organization did, how everyone performed on the priorities they said they were going to do, and then we reset for the new quarter. Apart from establishing foundational elements such as core values and core purpose, each quarterly session follows the same central process: where we are now, where do we want to go, what do we need to do to get there, and what could get in our way.

PETRA GROWTH ROADMAP OVERVIEW		YEAR 1				YEAR 2			
		QTR 1	QTR 2	QTR 3	QTR 4	QTR 1	QTR 2	QTR 3	QTR 4
PLANNING	Annual Planning Day: Senior leadership team	●				●			
	Quarterly Planning Day: Leadership team	●	●	●	●	●	●	●	●
	Rockefeller Habits Checklist Exercise			●				●	
MEETING RHYTHMS	Align: Daily updates of Huddle, Top Priority, Priorities, Tasks and KPI's	●	●	●	●	●	●	●	●
	Daily Huddle: Daily in-person 15-minute meeting	●	●	●	●	●	●	●	●
	Weekly Leadership Meeting: Review Priorities & Strategic Thinking	●	●	●	●	●	●	●	●
	Two-Week Top Task Reviews: Team members meet with managers		●	●	●	●	●	●	●
	Monthly Meeting			●	●	●	●	●	●
	Weekly Update of Critical Numbers	●	●	●	●	●	●	●	●
	Monthly Update of 1-Year & Quarterly Targets	●	●	●	●	●	●	●	●
	Leadership team attends Gazelles Summit	Attend Gazelles Growth and/or Leadership Summit				Attend Gazelles Growth and/or Leadership Summit			
ONE-PAGE STRATEGIC PLAN (OPSP)	Core Purpose & Core Values	●							
	Actions to keep "Alive" Core Purpose & Core Values			●		●		●	
	3-5 Year Targets & Key Thrusts/Capabilities	●							
	1-Year Targets & Annual Initiatives	●				●			
	Organization Quarterly Targets, Quarterly Priorities & Critical Numbers	●	●	●	●	●	●	●	●
	Individual Quarterly Priorities, Tasks & KPI's	●	●	●	●	●	●	●	●
	Theme			●	●	●	●	●	●
	Core Customer		●						
	Core Competencies		●						
	People & Process Drivers					●			
	7 Strata — Words You Own (Mindshare)			●					
	7 Strata — Sandbox		●						
	7 Strata — Brand Promise & Brand Promise KPI's			●					
	7 Strata — Brand Promise Guarantee (Catalytic Mechanism)			●					
	7 Strata — One-Phrase Strategy (Key to Making Money)							●	
	7 Strata — Differentiating Activities (3-5 How's)						●		
	7 Strata — X-Factor (10x-100x Underlying Advantage)						●		
	7 Strata — Profit per X (Economic Engine)			●					
	7 Strata — Big Hairy Audacious Goal (BHAG) 10-25 Year Goal		●						
	Strengths, Weaknesses, Opportunities & Threats/Trends (SWOT)	●		●					
	Balance Metrics		●				●		
ROCKEFELLER HABITS	Talent Assessment Exercise	●				●			
	One Page Personal Plan: Leadership team	●				●			
	Function Accountability Chart (FACe) & Metrics (KPI's) for leadership team		●				●		
	Process Accountability Chart (PACe) & Quarterly Process improvements	●	●	●	●	●	●	●	●
	DiSC – Internal communication training								
	TopGrading (Build scorecards and interviewing process)			●		●			
	Net Promoter Score (NPS) – Customer feedback loop					●			
	Employee Net Promoter Score (eNPS) – Employee feedback loop			●					
	Labor Efficiency Ration (LER)		●						
	Cash Acceleration Strategies (CASh) Exercise		●				●		
	Cash Fundability Exercise			●					●
	Cash: Power of One Exercise							●	
PETRA ENGAGEMENT	Engagement Service Level Agreement (SLA)	Kilimanjaro	Kilimanjaro	Kilimanjaro	Kilimanjaro	Kilimanjaro	Kilimanjaro	Denali	Denali
	Monthly Leadership Check-In's by Primary Coach	●	●	●	●	●	●	●	●
	6 Team Check-In's on RH Rhythms and OPSP assignments by Coach / CC	●	●	●	●	●			
	Weekly Accountability Report sent to all team members	●	●	●	●	●	●	●	●
	Ongoing monitoring of Company/Individual Priorities, Tasks & KPI's	●	●	●	●	●			

Legend: ● Completed During Planning ※ Team Assignment During Quarter

Petra Coach's implementation roadmap used to guide, quarter over quarter, the implementation of the Rockefeller Habits. ©2018 Petra Coach

CHECK-INS

In between those quarterly sessions, the lead coach does a monthly leadership check-in to see how things are going, either setting up the calls in advance or allowing the organization leader to be proactive about the call—whichever works best.

At the same time, the coach or the accountability coach is reaching out to team members to check in on quarterly strategic plan assignments—pieces of the Rockefeller Habits that team leaders are working on to provide assistance, guidance, and accountability.

Altogether, there are as many as eight structured check-ins every quarter, along with a weekly accountability report that goes out every Sunday to each person in the organization with everyone's priorities and how they've progressed … or not.

This is where the Align software plays one of its most important roles.

Because members are actively keeping their data updated in Align, an organization's coach has quick insight into what's happening or not happening at the member organization. There are times when our coaches have been able to coach without a phone call. They just review the Align software, evaluate what's going on, and then record a quick audio or video saying, "Hey, here's what I see going on. Do this."

This not only allows coaches to work on assessments at normally inaccessible times—like on an airplane or at 3 a.m.—but it also allows them to be more proactive in their review instead of almost reactive when it comes to talking on the phone.

It's a lot of transparency and accountability, and that's exactly what we're shooting for with our coaching and software. People want to know what's going on and this gives them a real-time snapshot of exactly where the organization stands on achieving both its short-term and long-term priorities.

KEEPING A CONSTANT RHYTHM

One of the more difficult, yet most important parts of the Rockefeller Habits methodologies to maintain is keeping the meeting rhythms alive and relevant. Every meeting may not be the *best* use of everyone's time, but they should always be a *good* use of everyone's time, from the daily and weekly huddles, to the "tweekers" or two-weekers and monthlies.

Core values and core purpose are another constant drumbeat. You may post the words around the office and make little notecards with your values and purpose on them, but that's not enough. Core values and purpose need to become top of mind with everyone at the organization. Team members should know the words, but they should also understand clearly what they mean and how to express them. In other words, everyone must live the values daily.

Implementing the Habits takes effort, a lot of it, but it's worth every second. The same is true for every organization

I've ever worked with, including my own—and the payoff is exponentially rewarding.

At the very beginning, when we first started implementing the Rockefeller Habits at NationLink, no one wanted to step away from the massive amount of work we had to do, the ringing phones and streaming emails, and spend time thinking about what's working, what's next, and how we are going to get there.

But I knew it was necessary for me to keep my sanity as the leader of a fast-growth organization. I knew the Rockefeller Habits were what we needed to do because we had to do something different. Something had to change.

Fear or frustration—one or both of these is going to be your impetus. That's when change happens. ❧

WHAT OUR MEMBERS ARE SAYING

"You'd be better today if you started with Petra Coach yesterday! We were a successful company that was growing even without a vision or goals. When we started the quarterly planning sessions we didn't realize the immediate impact it would have on our people and company. We eclipsed our three-year goals in the second year. Now we are setting targets and goals we wouldn't have dreamed of when we first starting working with Petra Coach."

CHAPTER 5: KEY TAKEAWAYS

It's not easy to take time away from your busy work schedule to plan for the day, quarter, and year, but it's necessary if your business is going to make the Habits work.

Candidate companies for Petra Coach services must be:

- **Personal Growth-Oriented.** Leaders have to be personally committed to changing themselves before others.

- **Willing to Reproduce Themselves.** Leaders must be willing to share information so others can take on responsibilities.

- **Able to Commit to Application.** Leaders must be willing to take what they learn and immediately apply it to themselves.

- **In the Right Mind-Set.** Either so frustrated with their business that they're willing to do anything to change it, or fearful of a missed opportunity.

The first planning session begins with the executive leadership team on the first day, and the second day includes upper management and, in some cases, the whole organization. The second day of planning is about accomplishing goals, not simply reviewing them.

Petra Coaching and the Align software are all about transparency and accountability. We're about providing a real-time snapshot of exactly where the organization stands on achieving both its long- and short-term priorities.

THE SHORT VERSION

PETRA COACH
CASE STUDIES

The following case studies, with anecdotes and information provided by the individual companies, are where you're going to find hard numbers and specific examples of how Petra Coach has helped a broad range of member companies. Some of these may not be directly relevant to you, but together, they show how Petra Coach and the Rockefeller Habits work for any organization of any size.

PETRA COACH IMPACT REPORT

EACH YEAR WE GATHER DATA TO MEASURE THE RESULTS OUR MEMBER COMPANIES HAVE EXPERIENCED

72
NPS
NET PROMOTER® SCORE

85%

OF LEADERSHIP TEAMS HAVE MORE TIME
TO WORK "ON THEIR BUSINESS" VS. "IN THEIR BUSINESS"

"Having goals and clear action plans have made it easier to engage the team to drive more of the initiatives verses being so in the weeds with it."
— **Ben Rigsby** | SnapShot Interactive

"We are more focused as an organization since working with Petra and as a result, we are getting more done. I have grown as a leader and I have a better understanding of what it is going to take to scale my company. If you want to grow your company, you will move faster by hiring Petra."
— **Tom Bemiller** | The Aureus Group

"This process has helped me become laser focused on what matters the most to my business."
— **Shawn Rubel** | Eezy

87% OF LEADERS

FEEL THEY HAVE MADE POSITIVE STEPS
TO CREATE A TRUE CULTURE SINCE BEGINNING TO WORK WITH PETRA

INCREASED REVENUE BY 24.2%

"This has TRANSFORMED our business. It's like owning an entirely different company, which is exactly what I was wishing for once we started."
— **Ben Holliday** | Mazurek & Holliday PC.

"My tolerance for B and C players has substantially lessened. We are attracting better talent and removing dead weight quicker. My A players are more invested, leading, and collaborating and we are operating better under the 'we' vs 'me' mentality."
— **Julie Scates** | J2T Recruiting

10% INCREASE IN PROFITS $

The Bradford Group

"We have learned to be comfortable talking about our Core Values all the time. And our Quarterly Themes are causing them to come alive in our organization".
— **Jay Clarke** | Renew Co.

40% INCREASE IN TEAM MEMBER ENGAGEMENT

5.48 AVG PRIOR / 7.67 AVG AFTER
(ON A SCALE OF 0-10)

CHAPTER 6

NATIONLINK

Gross Margin 4x Industry Average

T his may sound crazy, but in some regards the Rockefeller Habits saved my life.

This system, or methodology if you will, gave me
the ability to see that I needed to be a different person
to run NationLink. They gave me insight into my organization
by creating systems, processes, and meeting rhythms and forced
me to sit down and create a vision of the organization that I could
clearly communicate to the group of really smart people who
worked with me. And at the time I was so buried in my own way
of thinking that I truly didn't realize how smart they were.

During the first phase of NationLink, before we sold it
and took it back again, my wife Nicole and I ran everything.
We ran it hard and fast, making all the decisions. We bought
all the inventory, knew what was in stock, and knew what
was selling. It was easy, but again, there were only a few of us.
As we grew, however, that control and clarity of process was
more difficult to maintain. Just as Verne says in *Rockefeller
Habits*, "the complexity of an organization exponentially
multiplies as additional people come into an organization."

That complexity was a surprise for me then and again
when I started Petra Coach, and I know it surprises other

people today. I don't know why the hell we're surprised by it, because we teach others that it's going to happen, but when it does, we're still shocked.

As Verne points out, "It doesn't matter who you are and what you do; it's how you react and manage it that's important."

> **WHAT OUR MEMBERS ARE SAYING**
>
> "I feel better about the business and where it is going. I feel like I have more control over outcomes."

The discovery of the Rockefeller Habits, and actually walking through the implementation process, fundamentally changed me as a leader of the NationLink organization and fundamentally changed how we conducted our day-to-day business from that point on—but first I had to learn to accept the wisdom and advice of those who came before me.

THE CORE OF NATIONLINK

Core Values

✓ **Easy**—Make it easy for clients to do business with us and easy for us to do that business.

✓ **Experts**—Ensure we have the knowledge, tools, and solutions to always lead in our fields and continually grow.

✓ **Enthusiastic**—Be enthusiastic in everything we do and make it fun.

Core Purpose

✓ Making Wireless Easy!

Big Hairy Audacious Goal

✓ To change the way wireless is purchased and used in the US by empowering technology backed by the e3 Guarantee.

RIP OFF AND DUPLICATE

Speaker Cameron Herold has a great saying about the acronym "R&D."

"R and D isn't 'research and development,'" he says, "It's 'rip off and duplicate.'"

You don't have to come up with something new all on your own to change your business. A lot of the time, all the information you need is already out there. That's why Verne constantly reiterates the value of reading. He said it so much at that first EO seminar I attended back in the early 2000s that I thought, "All right, I give. I'll do it."

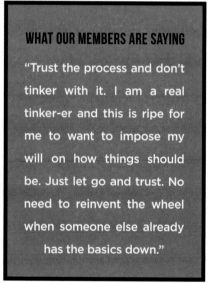

WHAT OUR MEMBERS ARE SAYING

"Trust the process and don't tinker with it. I am a real tinker-er and this is ripe for me to want to impose my will on how things should be. Just let go and trust. No need to reinvent the wheel when someone else already has the basics down."

As it turned out, those really smart people who came before me in the business world knew what they were talking about. I got heavily into reading and started R&D-ing. With the Rockefeller Habits as my base, I began looking at what pieces I could borrow from those who had gone before me that would improve my business and improve me.

EARLY STRUGGLES

In chapter 3, I spoke to the frustrations our whole team shared around implementing the daily huddle. Everyone had work to do—the phones were ringing, emails were piling up—and here I was, forcing them to walk away from their desks and spend fifteen minutes sharing in a circle.

But we didn't give up. Change was a matter of perseverance, not just flipping a switch. It's like someone who's overweight and desperately wants to change, so he or she picks up the kettlebells once or goes for one run and expects to suddenly be a new person.

Persistence, I'd learned, is what makes the Rockefeller Habits pay off, and I would not let them go.

In all, it took about three years for us to make everything into a habit. It took a few months to get the flywheel of implementation going, but *starting* was the biggest hurdle. It felt like an interruption in our day, sitting around in a planning session talking about what needed to be executed on, implementing the meeting rhythms, working on brand promise, and creating core values. No one wanted to give up that time, and it didn't feel like it was going much of anywhere at first.

That's why the two factors of either being incredibly frustrated or incredibly fearful about where your business is or where it may be headed are key. You have to know that where you are is not where you need to be, and that change absolutely has to occur.

I was fortunate enough to have a great team that was ultimately up for following and leading through the process of implementing the Rockefeller Habits. Making sure everyone showed up to the meetings and had good, relevant content wasn't easy at first, but that's a constant battle with every organization out there today. As sales coach Jack Daly puts it, "The urgent tends to crowd out the important." We had to realize that and purposefully work to put the important first.

At first, we did the quarterly sessions ourselves. Over time we found a third party that allowed me to participate in rather than lead the day, and I learned about the importance of being thoughtful in creating where we were going in a year or three years and what we had to get done in a quarter to get there.

Early on, the creation of core values and core purpose gave us a cultural foundation that was incredibly important, and we soon learned the incredible importance of the Topgrading[5] hiring process—a methodology created by organizational psychologist Dr. Brad Smart and an R&D that's now a living part of the Rockefeller Habits.

BUILDING THE HIRING PROCESS

The ability to be really thoughtful in interviewing and reviewing someone for a position at NationLink was huge for us. It was also incredibly arduous. Nobody wanted to

---

5   The practice of creating the highest quality workforce by ensuring that talent acquisition and talent management processes focus on identifying, hiring, promoting, and retaining high performers, A Players, in the organization at every salary level. (www.topgrading.com)

do Topgrading, but then again, nobody really wants to do any of this stuff at first. But we don't do these things for the process—we do them for the result.

And once we started, we got pretty good at it, even sending a few people up to Topgrading headquarters in Chicago for certification. We documented our interview process and implemented all the practices that Topgrading recommended.

There were many times when a team member and I would be two and a half hours into an interview and we'd both be thinking, "Dang, this is a long time to be in

> **WHAT OUR MEMBERS ARE SAYING**
>
> "I value our team more now than ever and realize just how important great people are. Hire great people and then get out of their way. Before Petra, I somewhat tried to do it all myself or at least wanted to be involved in most decisions. It wasn't scalable."

an interview." But not one hire that went through the process came to us later and asked us why we took up so much of their time. Instead, they told us how thoughtful it was and how impressed they were that we didn't let just anyone in the door.

From the potential hires' perspective, this process was a way for them to learn about what we did and how we did it, and it helped them decide if our organization felt like a good fit and vice versa. Topgrading gave us the ability to get hiring *right*, which was ultimately a cornerstone of our success.

BAD WORDS

At NationLink, language was a very big part of our culture. The words you use have an impact, so we borrowed an idea from sales trainer Tom Hopkins, training our team to replace "bad words" with more neutral or even positive ones.

We didn't say "problem," for instance—we said "challenge." We didn't say, "try," we said, "I will." And we'd test people on it. In the beginning, we'd give them a sheet with all the bad words on it and their replacements, and they'd have to memorize it. Then we'd quiz them and everyone had to get a score of one hundred or they'd have to retake the test until they did. We'd pull out pop quizzes in the middle of huddles, too, until the replacement words became engrained.

It's amazing how powerful our weird little language became. Even years later, I still run into people I worked with back then and they tell me how it still makes them cringe when they hear one of the "bad words."

Savings	Reduce overspending; Eliminate unnecessary spending
Price	Investment
Down payment	Initial investment
Monthly payment	Monthly investment
Contract	Agreement; paperwork
Buy	Own
Sell	Get them involved
Deal	Opportunity
Sign	Approve; Autograph; Okay
Pitch	Presentation
Objections	Area of concern

Cheap	Inexpensive
Customers	Clients
Try	I will
Prospect	Future client
Problems	Challenges
Appointment	Visit
But	And
Credit check	Preapproval

Today in our coaching practice we've identified several leadership bad words. Language can swing a conversation, increase understanding and even inspire. A handful of common ones we work on with teams are:

Can't	How can I/we
Me/I	We
For	With (ex. "working for" vs. "working with")
My	Our
But	And
Direct report	Direct support
Employee	Teammate; Coworker
Manager	Coach; Mentor
Work/life balance	Work/life purpose

And one of my all-time pet peeves...

To be honest...	N/A (Why would you need to clarify when you are being honest? Just stop saying this altogether.)

QUARTERLY THEMES

Another aspect of the Rockefeller Habits that I had to take on good faith at the beginning was the quarterly themes. In the back of my mind, I questioned the idea of putting all this time and effort into something that didn't appear to directly impact our bottom line, but it was part of the Habits. So we did it.

"Lemons to Lemonade" was one of our very first themes and reflected our work around client service. Client service with wireless carriers has never been a core competency for them, so we prided ourselves on how you could call our department and we would do everything we could to solve your challenge.

As a wireless sales and marketing business, we dealt with cell phones every day. So you can imagine that no one ever called us to say, "Hey, just wanted to let you know that my cell phone is working great." It just didn't happen.

Instead, it was a constant stream of, "This is broken. This isn't working. My bill is wrong. I lost my charger. My screen is cracked."

"Lemons to Lemonade" became our way of telling stories about unhappy clients—lemons—and how we overcame their challenges and turned them into "lemonade." We didn't just tell the stories, either; we made them visual.

Each story was written on a cutout of a lemon, and during our weekly team meeting, team members would tell their lemon-to-lemonade story. We kept fresh lemonade in the lobby during the entire quarter and we even had a lemon tree. We had lemons everywhere for three months, and at the end of the quarter, we had a lemon-themed celebration.

We always did some level of celebration for each quarter, based on a measurable outcome. For example, we wanted 250 lemon-to-lemonade stories in the quarter, so the award for reaching that number was a group trip to a baseball game with the families—we even had lemonade and a few beers.

We repeated this every quarter, coming up with a new theme every ninety days, and even though not every one was a home run, they were all great for building organizational culture—and by making it fun, we also accomplished a lot of big priorities with our themes.

ROCKEFELLER HABITS FROM THE TEAM MEMBER'S POINT OF VIEW

"Mandy Burage is one of our longest-running team members. She's worked with me for more than a decade, starting at NationLink in 2005 and becoming our first full-time team member at Petra Coach in 2012. If anyone can speak to the impact of the Rockefeller Habits, both on NationLink and on me personally, it's her."

—Andy

I started at NationLink right after I graduated from college, and at first, it was like any other business out there. You'd come into work, go to your desk, and just start working.

I was selling cellular services at first and didn't have all that much interaction with Andy, which was fine with me because Andy was really intimidating. He was leading the business through a big growth phase and had this presence that made it a little frightening to approach him—especially as a young employee. I still remember days when I would see him coming down the hall and immediately drop my head and get to one side just to get out of his way.

Then my manager left and I took over that position, which required me to work with Andy directly. Again, he was intimidating, but this was also right when he'd just gotten back from his first Birthing of Giants class. Suddenly he was all about the Rockefeller Habits process and how we were going to implement them, and I was on the team that would be pushing out these new methodologies to the organization.

We started holding leadership meetings, creating our one-page plan, and kicking off the meeting rhythms, and even though none of us really knew what we were doing, we all felt like we were in it together. Andy was our first coach, even though he was learning it right along with us. He'd take us through exercises that forced us to look at long-term goals, which was something we hadn't considered much as a business, and what we would be doing in the next week, next month, and next quarter to get there.

Where our organization was going to be three-to-five years from then was also new to us. Andy had probably thought about it, of course, but that's not something that leaders really think to share, so it was incredible to sit with our team and think about things beyond the day-to-day and how we were going to accomplish them.

That was the key for us—doing it all as a team. It was tough at first, but after a while it really became ingrained in our culture. Today, I don't even know how to start a day without a huddle! And it changed Andy, too. He became much more approachable, and after a while, I not only felt like I could talk to him about anything, but I greatly respected him as a mentor.

But as much as the Rockefeller Habits helped Nation-Link, and even Andy, one thing that I can speak to now, from the coaching perspective, is that the Habits aren't for everyone. The Rockefeller Habits bring a level of accountability that doesn't allow you to just skate by or disappear at your desk, not really getting any work done. When you implement something like the Rockefeller Habits, there are suddenly goals that need to be hit and metrics and reporting enforcing them. Everyone is accountable for making these things happen, so if you're not doing the work, then it becomes pretty obvious, pretty quickly.

The daily huddle was so important to us that it even became a part of the interview process. We'd have our candidates attend a huddle so they could see how they would have to stand in front of the entire organization every morning and report on what they did or didn't do the day before and what they would be working on that day. If that wasn't their cup of tea, then we both knew that NationLink wasn't the place for them.

That accountability became a big part of our culture, because we knew we could rely on one another to get things done. We celebrated our daily wins and we celebrated with our quarterly themes, as well as other fun little things that probably seemed a little strange to people on the outside.

I say that because I would tell my friends about what we did—like the lemons-to-lemonade quarterly theme, doing cheers at meetings, and decorating the office for any number of reasons—and they would tell me that they didn't do any of that at their jobs. It made me feel kind of special, to know I was a part of an organization that did these things when no one else did.

It was unique and it made me stay at NationLink, because the day-to-day job wasn't that glamorous. I mean, I was selling cell phones—you can do that anywhere, right? But the culture made a not-so-cool job seem really cool. I felt like I was a part of something greater. I could actually participate in planning sessions and knew I was being heard, whereas friends of mine with jobs that seemed cool on the surface were just numbers that got constantly overlooked. It meant a lot to me, and it's why I stayed on for so long—much longer than most young, straight-out-of-college employees.

—Mandy Burage, COO of Petra Coach
and Accountability Coach

SURVIVING THE 2008 RECESSION

A quarterly theme actually ended up being a significant revenue saver for our organization. It was during the housing market bubble burst in 2008 when clients were shutting off cell phones left and right as their companies downsized and employees were being fired by the thousands. Our revenue was taking a serious hit, so we turned to the *Rockefeller Habits*—specifically, to a section called "4Q Conversations."

What 4Q essentially means is, "What are the four questions that you should call your clients and ask?" These questions are:

1. How are you doing?

2. How is your industry doing?

3. Are you hearing from our competitors?

4. How are we doing and is there anything we need to do better?

Asking these questions, Verne wrote, should be considered an investment in customer retention. "If companies were able to hold on to the customers they now lose from neglect," wrote Verne, "it would fuel at least half their growth."

It was an interesting takeaway and one, I thought, that would make a great quarterly theme. We called it "200 4Q Conversations" and it took place during the fourth quarter of 2008.

That theme helped our business a ton. It wasn't a priority, necessarily, but we knew these companies were in trouble. Our customers were out there hurting, and instead of us calling them trying to wring more money out of them, we were just checking to see how they were doing.

We'd ask, "How's your industry?"

"Man, it sucks right now," they might say. "We're going through a downsizing, we had to lay off twenty guys last week."

It wasn't something that other companies were doing—we weren't making them pay their bills, we were asking how we could help. More often than not, we'd offer to suspend a line of service for them, which helped them avoid disconnect penalties on lines they weren't using, saving them money and saving us from having to pay back any commission we'd made by selling those lines in the first place. It was a win-win all around, but we wouldn't have known to offer that option if we hadn't made those 4Q calls.

HABITS AND EFFICIENCY PAY OFF

When we first sat down to write out our one-page plan in 2003/2004, we had a general feel for where our industry was and what our competitors were doing. This was because we received regular reports from our carriers that stated how many activations had been made in a given time period and who'd activated them.

Then, since everyone received the same commission for each activation, and we had a general idea of how many retail locations each of our competitors had, we were able to come up with some rough but fairly accurate comparisons.

What that meant in developing our one-page plan was that we could use these numbers to set a high yet achievable goal for NationLink—which is known as "profit per x" in the Rockefeller Habits. For us, that turned out to be "Creating an organization that has 2x the gross margin of the industry."

When we set that goal, our gross margin number was about equal to the rest of the industry: about $75,000 per full-time employee (FTE). But by writing down that one metric of increasing our gross margin per FTE by two times the industry average, we became uber-focused on efficiency—to the point where we were constantly looking for ways to do more with the same or less effort. We didn't even consider hiring a new team member until it became absolutely necessary.

That wasn't our only approach, of course. We also made it a point to constantly look at ways we could reinvent the way we did business, making it more efficient so that we could rely on technology or systems and processes instead of leveraging new people.

For instance, we knew the pain and cost of running brick-and-mortar stores. We had a bunch of them in retail and even mall settings, and we had to carry the costs for all of those, from staffing to inventory to costs of the property itself.

Over the course of time, however, we systematically closed all those retail shops and moved almost entirely to business-to-business sales. Instead of an entire store, we had one sales rep working out of a small office who turned over pretty much the same number of line activations as a retail location.

But we never would have thought of that if we hadn't focused on how we were going to hit that metric of moving up the gross margin per person.

Another thing we did was create an online selling platform for cell phones, which was built specifically for large businesses.

At the time, most major corporations offered a discount for cell-phone service, but few employees were aware of the benefit or of what products they were eligible to get the discount on.

What we did, then, was call the human resources department in all these major companies and tell them, "Look, your employees get a 20 percent discount on their cell phones. It's a work benefit for them. Wouldn't you like to have a place where they could go and order phones online and receive that discount?"

For those that said yes, we set up a customized version of our web platform, which we called the Employee Value Program, or EVP for short, and gave HR flyers to pass out with links to their custom site. When employees placed orders, we had a team that took care of the specifics and made sure the discounts were processed through the carrier. If someone had a challenge with a bill, he or she could call us and we'd handle it instead of having to go through the carrier's customer service.

It was phenomenal. Employees were getting better benefits; major companies were happy with our services, even bringing us on for more services; and when we finally sold the organization, that division alone accounted for a major share of what we sold the whole organization for.

By the time we sold the organization, we'd shot that 2x gross margin of the industry metric right out of the water. As of the day we sold in 2011, our gross margin per full-time employee was $275,000—nearly 4x the industry average. And we never would have done it if we hadn't looked beyond the curve, putting systems and processes in place to help us reach what we all thought was a pretty audacious goal. ❧

NATIONLINK: CASE STUDY TAKEAWAYS

You don't have to come up with something new all on your own to change your business—the information you need is usually already out there.

Read—because those really smart people who came before you in the business world knew what they were talking about.

Change is a matter of perseverance.

It took three years for NationLink to entirely embrace the Rockefeller Habits.

In setting that one metric, we suddenly became uber-focused on efficiency—to the point where we were constantly looking for ways to do more with the same or less effort.

The Habits aren't for everyone—they bring a level of accountability that doesn't allow people to fly under the radar—but for those who implement them, they can help you reach some pretty audacious goals.

cators (KPIs), but it works. We videoconference our teams in from Kentucky and Missouri, all of us surrounding our monitors to share our big 'I wills' for the day," said Mark.

"The daily huddles are another thing that separates us from other digital marketing agencies," said Ben. "It gives us a rigid morning structure, and for creative agencies, that's rare."

THE SNAPSHOT HUDDLE STRUCTURE

And it is a pretty rigid schedule. Each day at SnapShot Interactive begins with an 8:15 a.m. meeting of the project managers, in which they review needs and any possible scheduling conflicts from shoot standpoints, launch dates, or other products.

At 8:30, the web team meets. The team members go through all their open projects in about fifteen minutes— quite a feat when the list can include over two hundred open projects.

At 8:46, the entire team does a daily standup in which they share good news and one thing each person plans to get out the door that day in regard to their KPIs.

Finally, at 9:00, the video and animation team meets to go through all *their* open projects.

And then the day starts.

"Early on, we would sit in on all of the huddle meetings, but as the culture grew, other people started taking the lead," said Mark. "We're reducing the need for us to be involved in everything."

QUARTERLY MEETINGS FOR EVERYONE

Ben and Mark, however, *do* like to push team members to be involved in as many aspects of the organization's planning as possible. Even with more than fifty team members and growing, Mark and Ben continue to include everyone in their quarterly meetings, with the Petra Coach team leading the day, taking the entire team away from the office for a day to implement the Rockefeller Habits, set goals, and review past achievements.

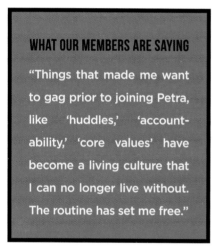

WHAT OUR MEMBERS ARE SAYING

"Things that made me want to gag prior to joining Petra, like 'huddles,' 'account-ability,' 'core values' have become a living culture that I can no longer live without. The routine has set me free."

"I'd probably say that the huddles and meeting repetitions have impacted our business the most," said Mark. "Even in the quarterly meetings, our team will set these goals that sometimes Ben and I think are going to be incredibly difficult to take on in a quarter's time, but they pull it off.

"We've found that when our team members set the goals and we create ownership for them, then anything is possible. We've moved the organization really far, really fast due to these quarterly planning meetings that everyone is contributing to, and that involvement rolls right down into all of our daily rhythm meetings," Mark added.

Another side benefit of including the entire team in organizational planning is the way it instills a sense of accountability in each and every team member.

"Clients visiting our shop have commented on it a lot; that there's such an energy and enthusiasm around what we're doing, such a sense of ownership, even when we're not around," said Mark.

The reason, Mark and Ben explained, is because the whole team is involved in making big decisions for the organization. Not only that but once they've made those decisions, then they take them on—they *own* them.

"I'd say there are very few agencies out there that have moved their businesses as fast as we have and done as good a job in scaling up from two to fifty people in such a short time," said Mark.

COMFORTABLE WITH TRANSPARENCY

Another Habit that was a challenge for SnapShot to implement—but also one of the most beneficial—was transparency.

"My fear was that if our creative team knew about all of our business challenges and financial information and learned that we'd missed the mark on a goal, they might jump ship," said Ben. "But what happened was the exact opposite. Whether we miss a goal or exceed one, the team rallies around and figures out how we can move faster or how we can improve. It's not Mark and me trying to put solutions in place and guiding everyone. It's the team saying, 'Okay guys, here's how we missed the target. Here's what we're going to do starting today to move the needle in the opposite direction.' That's really been the fun of these meetings—watching this happen. It kind of takes the pressure off."

HURRICANES AND INTERACTIVE ART

The quarterly meetings with Petra Coach are a prime incubator for creating the agency's upcoming quarterly themes. It's the last activity of the planning session and one of the most anticipated.

Each theme at SnapShot is created through friendly competition, with team members split into several different groups and given the challenge of coming up with the best theme based on the goals set by the organization's upcoming quarterly priorities. The themes are then presented and everyone votes on the best one, with the winning team taking ownership of implementing it during the upcoming quarter. Petra Coach calls this "Theme Team Wars."[7]

"It helps that we've got a highly creative group of individuals," said Ben. "We all know the priorities we're working to accomplish, but there's no specific direction we have to go to achieve them. One group may go a certain direction while another takes a completely different approach. They really work on how to make it memorable and how everyone can be involved in it."

The carefully crafted ownership mentality of the SnapShot team members has also played well into achieving each quarterly theme's goal, with team members pushing one another to hit and exceed each mark.

With their "Making it Rain" theme, for instance, the team blew their goal number out of the water and were rewarded with a hurricane party, complete with hurricane drinks and an actual hurricane drink machine.

"With that theme, everyone in the organization got a raindrop whenever they made an introduction to a salesperson, like through a friend, family member, or someone in the community … anyone who might need our services or who might want to work with us one day," said Mark.

If a team member got five raindrops, he or she got a really nice SnapShot Interactive umbrella and the party was a reward for reaching the cumulative goal.

---

7   "Theme Team Wars" videos are available for viewing at the Petra Coach website at http://petra-coach.com/clients-saying/.

The theme was such a success that the agency has done a couple of variations on it since then, including a "Chip In" theme with poker chips to help drive the sales needle forward.

To encourage more interaction among team members, another recent theme centered around, "Will You Be My Friend," where individuals throughout the organization were encouraged to make connections and learn different things about one another.

"What we ended up with were a lot of really fun facts about one another, which we put together into an art piece with everyone's pictures on it with lines drawn between each of the individuals who made a connection," said Ben.

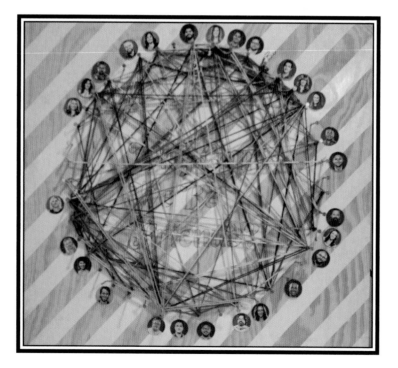

PERSONAL ACCOUNTABILITY

"Implementing the Rockefeller Habits and working with Petra Coach has truly been the difference between incremental improvements and vast improvements," said Ben. "The difference between success and failure, in some regards."

Having a third party keeping them personally accountable—someone who isn't in the day-to-day of SnapShot and who could look at their business compared to other businesses and give them some reference on how they're actually growing within their industry—has been invaluable, according to both Mark and Ben.

"We've built an incredible team and instituted more efficient processes than we've ever had before, but for us to fall in line with that, we needed accountability," said Mark. "It's just that level of accountability and transparency; it's been very successful for us."

"There are days we go into meetings with our coach and we just feel like we're going to get lambasted. But he comes in and picks us up and pushes us forward. That's exactly what you need in a coach, to help celebrate those wins," said Ben. "And I think the team really enjoys it when the coach really gives it to Mark and me sometimes. It's good to see that no one is beyond being held accountable."

Since SnapShot Interactive opened its doors six years ago, they've experienced 100+ percent year-over-year growth, and the team continues to shoot for that goal every year.

"Being able to share that level of ownership and feeling responsible for it creates unexpected experiences just by the nature of it," said Ben. "We want to use that capital as efficiently and as responsibly as we can in pushing the limit and giving more on a project to create that experience. It's how we build raving fans and how we continue to improve. We live to over-deliver inspirational solutions." ❧

SNAPSHOT INTERACTIVE: CASE STUDY TAKEAWAYS

SnapShot began with Petra Coach from practically day one, with only two employees—the owners, Ben and Mark. Today, SnapShot still involves fifty-plus members of the team in quarterly and annual planning.

The daily huddles were the hardest Habit to get going and keep going consistently, followed by the challenge of becoming comfortable with transparency. But because of it, team members have begun to contribute to finding ways to improve when they miss a mark.

Quarterly themes help with team interaction, encouraging connections, and helping to drive organization-wide goals.

Accountability was vital to SnapShot, helping them build an incredible team and institute more efficient processes than they ever had before.

Since SnapShot Interactive opened its doors in 2010, they've experienced 100+ percent year-over-year growth.

CHAPTER 8

APTIFY

Shifting to a Culture First Driven Organization

BUSINESS TYPE

Application software for enterprise-class associations, not-for-profits, and other member-based organizations

NUMBER OF EMPLOYEES:

250+

LOCATION:

Washington DC; Chicago, IL; New Orleans, LA; Pune, India; Sydney, Australia; Dublin, Ireland

A ptify began as a software organization in 1993, selling to large commercial organizations before founder Amith Nagarajan realized that the not-for-profit space was an amazing market that was drastically underserved. In the mid-1990s, Aptify switched to providing software specifically designed for enterprise-class associations, and before the turn of the millennium, his organization was recognized as an Inc. 500 company—twice.

"We'd grown and seen success, but we realized that we needed consistent, repeatable, scalable processes in place so that the management team would grow at the same rate as the business," said Amith. "At the same time, I knew that I had a real passion for helping these not-for-profit organizations change the world, but that deep rooted purpose wasn't truly alive in our culture. That was another thing the Habits did for us—they helped us clarify our core purpose and rebuild our entire culture around it."

Amith and I knew each other through the Entrepreneurs' Organization in Nashville, and it was around the same time that he found out about the new coaching business that he began reading *Mastering the Rockefeller Habits*.

"A friend of mine actually introduced me to the book, and when I started talking with him about it, he said I should go talk to Andy. So I connected with him, was impressed with his passion and vision for helping fellow entrepreneurs build their companies with the Habits, and we went from there," said Amith.

"WILL THIS WORK ON A GLOBAL SCALE?"

> ### WHAT OUR MEMBERS ARE SAYING
>
> "Over 60 percent of our team work from their home or a remote location. We must be very intentional about helping our team feel well connected and not 'on an island.' The structure Petra has brought with huddles, an annual meeting, quarterly meetings, monthly all-hands calls, a newsletter, book club, Core Purpose, and Core Values provides the multi-media, multi-frequency communications to help our team stay engaged and connected."

At first, the management team at Aptify was cynical about the new system and having a coach facilitating the process. No one knew me or knew about the Rockefeller Habits, and they were skeptical that the methodology would work for hundreds of employees on a global scale.

But I answered every question for them and explained what the process was able to do and how the Habits worked, regardless of organizational size. I also pushed the Aptify management team to adopt new thinking and was able to build momentum with the group over a short period of time.

"Ultimately, the thing about Andy is he knows this stuff cold, but he's also really good at reading people and building relationships with different personality types," said Amith. "So he was able to form a connection with each person on our team and find a way to help each one understand how this was going to benefit not only the organization but him or her as an individual."

PRIORITY REDUCTION

After the initial struggle to gain buy-in, the first big challenge of implementing the Habits was getting the Aptify management team to narrow down their priorities.

"Everyone always thinks that there are fifty different things that have to be done now, but the reality is that you *don't* get those fifty things done. You get one or two things, or maybe three things done," said Amith. "You can either choose to make the difficult decisions on the front end, choosing not to do forty-seven things because you're committed to three, or you can attempt to do all fifty things—and what ends up happening is that you only get two or three done, and they're not the priorities you would have chosen. They are typically the most urgent two or three items—not the most important ones."

It was a challenge, getting the team on board with making the hard decisions up front and acknowledging that they couldn't get everything done, but they were able to get there after a couple of quarters of planning sessions.

"It became an interesting debate because everyone had a different opinion on what the most important things were for the organization to do," said Amith. "It was particularly difficult because we came from an environment where we were used to working with a far greater scope of priorities."

It took almost a year for that mentality to eventually fade, to be replaced by the finer focus of fewer priorities.

DON'T "TRY," JUST "DO"

Another challenge for the Aptify team was clearing out the "weak language" and focusing on strong goals and firm dates for completion.

"When you say that you're going to 'try' to accomplish a goal by a certain time, that language undermines the strength of your resolve," said Amith. "So we had to learn to be really clear, saying things like, 'We *will* achieve *x* by this certain date.' It's a quantifiable goal by a specific date, and that gets everyone to align around it, which feeds into creating key performance indicators (KPIs) that are actually predictive of our ability to achieve that goal."

For instance, Amith explained, a common KPI at many companies is how many sales you've made or how many dollars in sales you've made. The problem with that as a KPI, however, is that it's a lagging indicator. You only know about the sales once it's happened.

Instead, the best KPIs are the ones that are leading or *predictive* indicators. They're not the outcome so much as the activities accomplished that will lead to the greater goal. An actual outcome might be $1 million in sales for the quarter, but the KPIs could be the achievement of milestones that will lead to that outcome.

Take the goal of losing weight, for example. Instead of making your goal weight your KPI, you make it "work out four times a week" or "work off an extra one thousand calories a week." These are leading indicators, because they tell you ahead of time if the outcome you intend to achieve is likely to materialize.

"KPIs are a difficult thing to get right, and that's probably one of the most powerful behavioral shifts in our culture that Petra Coach helped us make—looking for leading or predictive indicators," said Amith.

LAGGING AND LEADING INDICATORS

LAGGING INDICATORS are easy to measure but only indicate where you've been—they're similar to looking through the rearview mirror while driving a car. Lagging indicators are typically output oriented and only give you the results of your actions. They don't influence the outcome because they are the outcome.

A personal example of a lagging indicator is a goal to lose 20 pounds. Business examples of lagging indicators are revenue and profit.

LEADING INDICATORS are an important tool for effectively managing and hitting goals. Leading indicators are activities that you perform on a regular basis to reach the desired outcome (the lagging indicator). A personal example is working out four times per week (which leads to losing 20 pounds.) In business, calling five decision makers every day would lead to new revenue.

PLAYING FAIR

Another powerful change at Aptify as a result of Petra Coaching has been the growth of a culture of appreciation.

"Appreciation is something that no person can receive too much of, and most organizations are extremely poor at both giving and receiving appreciation. It's not something that most organizations, most leaders, or even most people do well," said Amith.

But it's something that Aptify now focuses on regularly. In fact, a recent quarterly theme revolved around appreciation and supercharged communication.

To participate, team members were asked to fill out a *FAIR* card (a printed appreciation card, one with each of Aptify's core values on it) every time they saw another team member living by the organization's core values. "FAIR," in this case, stands for the four Aptify core values: Flexible, Accountable, Innovative, and Responsive.

If a team member noticed someone come up with a better way of doing something, for instance, then he or she was encouraged to write them a note on a FAIR card saying, "Great job doing ABC task in a new way; great example of living #Innovative," and give it to them.

The goal for the quarter was a thousand cards distributed, which, with more than 250 employees, adds up to about four cards written each.

THE CORE OF APTIFY

Core Values

✓ **Flexible**—Seek out diverse and rich views and adapt quickly and continuously to see the best outcome.

✓ **Accountable**—Accountability 360: accountable to self, accountable to team, accountable to client, accountable to community. Each layer of accountability is bi-directional—e.g., team is accountable to each individual, just as each individual is accountable to the team.

✓ **Innovative**—Never stop learning. Never be satisfied with how things are done. Always seek to find a better way.

✓ **Responsive**—People want to know their concerns will be handled. Set clear and realistic expectations, and then deliver.

Core Purpose

✓ Changing the world, one client mission at a time.

Big Hairy Audacious Goal

✓ 1,000 Enterprises POWERED by Aptify.

"It was a great theme and a great way to practice appreciation and communication and to reinforce core values," said Amith. "Though, in retrospect, before we really started implementing the Habits, I thought core values were a bunch of nonsense, because so many companies pick values that are generic and meaningless. They just slap it on a nice-looking plaque, hang it on the wall in their conference room, and it just sits there, doing nothing.

"Now that I've seen good examples," he added, "and we've implemented ours at Aptify, I'd say that if I could, I would have established our core purpose and values much earlier."

LEADERSHIP IS A LEARNED SKILL

In all, the Rockefeller Habits have not only helped Aptify—which has successfully grown to more than twice the size it was in 2011, thanks in large part to Petra Coaching and the Habits—but it's also helped Amith grow personally as a leader and an entrepreneur.

"One aspect of what Petra Coach does is bring new ideas and concepts to their clients. They're always introducing me and others to new ideas through books, speaking opportunities, conferences, and similar learning experiences," said Amith. "And it's important to stay on top of these things. The whole idea of constantly learning and driving your leadership skills by improving them and actively working on them like you would work on any other skill is incredibly important.

"People think I'm a leader because I have twenty-plus years of experience doing it, but it's not about just being in that role. Leadership is a skill that needs to be practiced and refined constantly," he added.

According to Amith, the learning process has not only improved his own leadership but also that of his management team and many of the team members.

Five years after starting the Rockefeller Habits implementation process, Amith is still enjoying the benefit of working with Petra Coach.

"I've seen the organization evolve a lot over the last five years and the methodologies have continuously improved," said Amith. "I consider Petra Coach to be an integral part of our executive team." ❧

APTIFY: CASE STUDY TAKEAWAYS

Narrowing down the management team's priorities was one of the first big challenges—getting them to understand that they couldn't get everything done every day, but they could get a few things done well every day. This mentality took almost a year to integrate.

The Aptify team learned the value of getting KPIs right, which drove one of their most powerful behavioral shifts—developing KPIs that were leading indicators instead of lagging indicators.

Developing a culture of appreciation was also an influential and positive change for the organization.

The coaching process helped Amith grow as a leader and has improved the leadership qualities of his management team and many team members.

CHAPTER 9

GREENEARTH LANDSCAPE SERVICES

Team Unity across Offices and Cultural Barriers

BUSINESS TYPE

Full-service landscape maintenance and design

NUMBER OF EMPLOYEES

80+

LOCATION

Panama City Beach & Santa Rosa Beach, FL

"We were frustrated," said Jeremy Durgan, cofounder of GreenEarth Landscape Services. "Frustrated because our organization was failing to scale at the rate we wanted, because our team was disconnected and we were disconnected. We needed guidance and had no idea what to do."

When Jeremy and his business partner, Shawn Knight, founded GreenEarth Landscape Services in 2007, it was with the intention of creating something much more than just a typical landscaping organization.

"When most people think 'landscaping companies,' the first thing that comes to mind is usually a guy driving a truck with more dents in it than not, rolling up to a house and cutting the grass for twenty-five bucks," said Jeremy. "Most people in my own family still think that's what I do. We're so much more than that, but as an organization we were having a hard time articulating that and finding people who wanted the same goal. Turned out it wasn't because we were doing the wrong things, necessarily—it was because we didn't know how to ask the right questions."

An avid reader, Jeremy had read *Scaling Up,* the second edition of *Mastering the Rockefeller Habits,* and three pages into it, realized that this was the process he wanted to use.

"Everything I knew we needed was right there, but I had no idea how to do it," said Jeremy. "It was a massive undertaking that we needed guidance on; not only as entrepreneurs and business owners but as a team."

At first, Jeremy and Shawn attempted to get the Habits going on their own, taking bits and pieces and trying to implement them in a vision that they eventually realized they never clearly articulated to their team.

> **WHAT OUR MEMBERS ARE SAYING**
>
> "I felt like a lone soldier for fifteen years and it always felt very me versus we. This year I felt connected to my team and felt my team was connected to the business in a way I have never experienced. I don't feel lonely or in it alone anymore."

"Here's my business partner and me coming in to work, all excited about these processes, trying to get everyone up to the same level of thinking as we are—but we were the only ones who'd read the books," said Jeremy. "The rest of our team had no idea how to get on the same page as us and it just made us angry—not at them but at the general situation.

It was a real slap in the face to put effort into these things and consistently see them not work. But we knew it was only two peoples' fault: mine and my business partner's."

So they decided to go back to the source and dig up some resources for implementing the Habits. *Scaling Up* had several references in it to different people, companies, and organizations, and they looked into each one, eventually landing on Petra Coach.

"They asked all the right questions in all the right ways in our first call with them," said Jeremy. "And they were very direct about what they were looking for in us, which I thought was admirable. We all needed to be on the same page when it came to successfully growing our organization."

DAY ONE WITH GREENEARTH

The very first planning session was a rollercoaster of emotions for everyone at GreenEarth Landscape Services. The leadership team had done some financial-planning sessions together, so they were more or less on the same page when it came to working together. But they weren't just working with the leadership team during those first two sessions. For the second day, Jeremy and Shawn were challenged to bring as many people from the organization as possible.

"There were people there who'd never been a part of a planning session before, and I quickly learned a lot about my ability to communicate effectively with the team. Before that day, I thought I was clearly articulating what we did day-to-day all the way through to the bigger plan," said Jeremy. "What I learned, about two hours into that first group session, was that it was more like 15 percent or even 10 percent. That was a hard pill to swallow. Then I saw how many different pages my team was on. Sometimes it was more like completely different *books*! It was crazy and a difficult thing to finally see."

There was a little resistance during that team meeting, as people who had been working with the organization for years—some since they'd graduated from high school or college—were pushed well outside their comfort zones. For most of the larger team, work was work. There was little emotion behind it. After that session, however, people began to feel more like a part of the team.

"We had the most resistance in that first quarter of planning sessions," said Jeremy. "After the second quarter you could see that people were excited, but there were still some people who weren't quite there. By the third quarter, it was great to see everyone self-starting, getting involved, creating their priorities with the right intent, and generally being excited about the process."

"If you were to come up to my team members—pre-Petra Coach and Rockefeller Habits—and ask them what our organization did, they would tell you that we cut grass and planted trees. Now they'll tell you that we create opportunities for growth. They'll tell you about our core purpose and core values and that cutting grass and planting trees are just a byproduct of us creating these opportunities for growth," said Jeremy. "That was a really important turning point for us as a business and as a team."

THE CORE OF GREENEARTH LANDSCAPE SERVICES

Core Values

✓ **G**row with Each Other

✓ **R**esponsive Communication

✓ **O**wn It

✓ **W**in and Lose Together

✓ **T**ake the Extra Step

✓ **H**umility and Respect

Core Purpose

✓ Grow People—we create opportunities for growth.

Big Hairy Audacious Goal

✓ Using communication to rewrite the experience in the landscape journey.

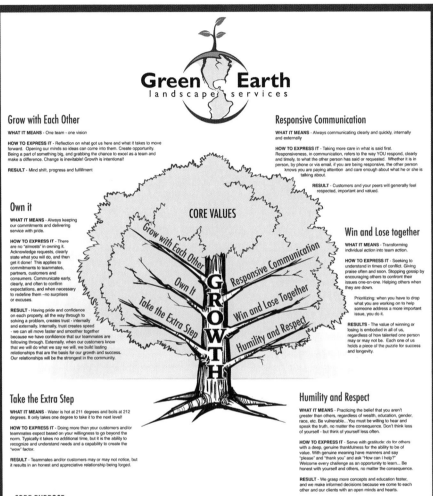

Green Earth
landscape services

Grow with Each Other

WHAT IT MEANS - One team - one vision

HOW TO EXPRESS IT - Reflection on what got us here and what it takes to move forward. Opening our minds so ideas can come into them. Create opportunity. Being a part of something big, and grabbing the chance to excel as a team and make a difference. Change is inevitable! Growth is intentional!

RESULT - Mind shift, progress and fulfillment

Responsive Communication

WHAT IT MEANS - Always communicating clearly and quickly, internally and externally

HOW TO EXPRESS IT - Taking more care in what is said first. Responsiveness, in communication, refers to the way YOU respond, clearly and timely, to what the other person has said or requested. Whether it is in person, by phone or via email, if you are being responsive, the other person knows you are paying attention and care enough about what he or she is talking about.

RESULT - Customers and your peers will generally feel respected, important and valued.

Own it

WHAT IT MEANS - Always keeping our commitments and delivering service with pride.

HOW TO EXPRESS IT - There are no "almosts" in owning it. Acknowledge requests, clearly state what you will do, and then get it done! This applies to commitments to teammates, partners, customers and consumers. Communicate early, clearly, and often to confirm expectations, and when necessary to redefine them –no surprises or excuses.

RESULT - Having pride and confidence on each property, all the way through to solving a problem, creates trust - internally and externally. Internally, trust creates speed - we can all move faster and smoother together because we have confidence that our teammates are following through. Externally, when our customers know that we will do what we say we will, we build lasting relationships that are the basis for our growth and success. Our relationships will be the strongest in the community.

CORE VALUES

Grow with Each Other
Responsive Communication
Own It
Win and Lose Together
Take the Extra Step
Humility and Respect

GROWTH

Win and Lose together

WHAT IT MEANS - Transforming individual action into team action.

HOW TO EXPRESS IT - Seeking to understand in times of conflict. Giving praise often and soon. Stopping gossip by encouraging others to confront their issues one-on-one. Helping others when they are down.

Prioritizing: when you have to drop what you are working on to help someone address a more important issue, you do it.

RESULTS - The value of winning or losing is embodied in all of us, regardless of how talented one person may or may not be. Each one of us holds a piece of the puzzle for success and longevity.

Take the Extra Step

WHAT IT MEANS - Water is hot at 211 degrees and boils at 212 degrees. It only takes one degree to take it to the next level!

HOW TO EXPRESS IT - Doing more than your customers and/or teammates expect based on your willingness to go beyond the norm. Typically it takes no additional time, but it is the ability to recognize and understand needs and a capability to create the "wow" factor.

RESULT - Teammates and/or customers may or may not notice, but it results in an honest and appreciative relationship being forged.

Humility and Respect

WHAT IT MEANS - Practicing the belief that you aren't greater than others, regardless of wealth, education, gender, race, etc. Be vulnerable…You must be willing to hear and speak the truth, no matter the consequence. Don't think less of yourself - but think of yourself less often.

HOW TO EXPRESS IT - Serve with gratitude: do for others with a deep, genuine thankfulness for the ability to be of value. With genuine meaning have manners and say "please" and "thank you" and ask "How can I help?" Welcome every challenge as an opportunity to learn… Be honest with yourself and others, no matter the consequence.

RESULT - We grasp more concepts and education faster, and we make informed decisions because we come to each other and our clients with an open minds and hearts.

CORE PURPOSE

Grow People – We create opportunities for growth

WHAT DOES IT MEAN? - It means always remembering what we do and why we do it each day.

Our core purpose:
To create opportunities for everyone to grow personally and professionally. Opportunity creates the moments for growth, which helps us achieve our core purpose.

HOW TO EXPRESS IT
Ask yourself, each other, customers and vendors: Does what we're about to do truly express our core purpose? If it does… own it! If it doesn't, reconsider. This applies to every decision we make: in customer service, hiring, workflow, etc.

RESULT - We grow together, creating an environment where everyone is more than just the business but a culture that grows in our lives both at work and home.

GreenEarth's core value grid showing each core value, what each means, how to express each, and what the result is when expressed. This is visually designed to match their culture.

180 DEGREES OF CULTURE

The quarterly theme, too, has been a very successful habit for GreenEarth.

"The themes were something I read about in *Scaling Up,* but I never really got how it would work until we were coached on it," said Jeremy. "Now it's huge! Everyone in the organization is involved and the majority of our team members get pretty excited about it."

The first theme GreenEarth took on was called "180 Degrees of Culture," which centered around collecting stories about other people in the organization who they'd seen engaged in a core value. On reaching the goal of 180 stories, the organization held a field day complete with games unique to the landscaping industry.

"We did mower races and a race where you had to use a backpack blower to maneuver a stress ball through this crazy obstacle course," said Jeremy, smiling. "And at the end we gave out prizes. It was a really fun day and it got a great response."

Another theme, "Mucho Hojas," or "lots of leaves," also focused on sharing stories about core values, but it involved sharing stories between locations at the same time, each week focusing on a different core value and writing those stories on paper leaves that they pinned to a large picture of the core-values tree.

"That way we were always talking *to* the other branch, talking *about* the other branch, and in general just being involved with each other, which will become even more important as we continue to expand our locations," said Jeremy.

One of the most impactful aspects of the quarterly themes, however, has been GreenEarth's dream-fulfillment program, a concept organized by John Ratliff when he ran Appletree Answers and one which Petra Coach introduced to the organization.

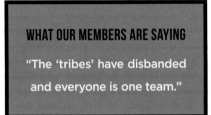

WHAT OUR MEMBERS ARE SAYING

"The 'tribes' have disbanded and everyone is one team."

With the dream-fulfillment program, each team member is asked to fill out a dream sheet with his or her dreams listed on it. Names are then placed in a hat and two people are selected to have their dreams fulfilled.

For the first drawing, one dream award went to a team member who'd always wanted to take his wife to a music and art festival in Texas but was never able to afford it. GreenEarth fulfilled that dream by giving him two tickets, VIP, to the event and covering the cost of their hotel.

"The response from him and the reward to us for being able to do that for him and his wife has been awesome," said Jeremy.

The second dream winner was a young man who was paying his own way through college, taking community college classes when he could. He was the first one in his family to go to college and he was proud of it, but he was in desperate need of a computer to do his schoolwork on and he couldn't afford one.

"Our dream fulfillment was to purchase him a computer to help with his education," said Jeremy. "It was great! Later, however, I heard that people were surprised that we actually followed through with fulfilling these dreams. That shocked me because as a business owner, I thought we followed through on everything, but apparently, we didn't. It was then that the point of the program really hit home with me. It built trust and created genuine happiness on the team."

Even though they weren't the first thing Jeremy and Shawn thought about when they began implementing the Rockefeller Habits, it turned out to be one of the most powerful Habits they've created.

Another Habit that began on day one, however, was a little more difficult for Jeremy and the team to undertake, and in some ways, even more personal.

"A TOUGH PIECE OF PAPER TO FILL OUT"

The One-Page Personal Plan, or OPPP, was an almost instant source of heartburn for Jeremy, as well as for several other members of the organization, because it specifically asked them to think about their business—and their lives—ten years out and to put some real thought into where they wanted to be. It wasn't something anyone could tell them, either. They found themselves considering what skills they needed to acquire, what they needed to become, and what they would need to know to make their OPPPs happen.

"That is a tough piece of paper to fill out," said Jeremy. "It's difficult to really come up with a solid and true answer when someone asks you, 'Where do you want your life to be ten, twenty years from now?' I still have managers in leadership that cannot finish that page, because it's just too much for them to focus on."

Three times a year the leadership team looks back on their OPPPs as a group and asks how it's going and what they're doing to accomplish their goals. It's a personal experience for each of them, as it communicates not only an interest in the team members' work but in their personal lives.

"The OPPP right out of the gate was a huge first step for our business, and it's helped a lot of us not only in our business life but personally, in our home lives, as well," said Jeremy.

It's also not a dormant document that you fill out and then leave in a drawer. Instead, it's actively referred to and revisions are encouraged. During GreenEarth's very next coaching session, in fact, the team was asked, "Now why is it going to take ten years to hit your OPPP goals?"

With that question in mind, Jeremy, along with several others, are now looking at how to make their ten-year goals happen in five years or less.

"That was just one page that's paid massive dividends in fulfillment and happiness. Without it, I'd never have found those goals. I wouldn't have done them and wouldn't think in the way that I think now versus the way I thought then. It's just a huge difference."

THE STRUGGLE WITH THE HUDDLE

Another Habit with a significant impact on GreenEarth was the daily huddle. With two office branches located about thirty-five miles from each other, it felt to the leadership team as though they were going in opposite directions and doing things completely different from each other. One branch often didn't want to work with the other and team relations were not going well.

At first, the struggle with the huddle was in making it meaningful. It brought everyone together, which was a great step in the right direction, but after a few months it began to turn into nothing more than a recitation of the daily schedule.

"We needed to be more engaged in the daily huddles as a whole, so we introduced a simple change suggested by Petra Coach," said Jeremy. "We made it so that everyone had to start their day by saying something they'd learned in the past twenty-four hours, whatever that may be. Putting that in there has made everything else we discuss much more valuable, because it encourages people to talk about their schedule in a little more detail. At the same time, it encourages others to ask questions, so by the end of it, everyone is clearly on the same page and knows what's going on."

Even with the greater detail, huddles at GreenEarth don't last longer than twelve minutes—but the impact, from leadership to frontline employee, has been powerful.

"Now with the daily huddle and using Aligntoday.com, we put our priorities for the quarter on a screen and talk about them every day," said Jeremy. "Our huddles are held at the exact same time at both branches via video conference, and the result has really helped bring everyone together. Daily huddles have really been the icing on the cake."

The weekly huddle, too, has helped bring the GreenEarth teams together, with team members taking that time to share their highs and lows, both personally and professionally.

"Just changing that terminology to include personal achievements and challenges was amazing," said Jeremy. "You hear the excitement everyone has when they talk about their children or their spouse or something they've done, and that excitement spills over into the team. They start caring about one another's highs or lows. It's such a simple thing but it's gone such a long way with the team."

"IT'S NOT ABOUT WHAT WE GET, IT'S WHO WE BECOME"

As GreenEarth progresses with the Habits, Jeremy, Shawn, and the rest of the leadership team are now regularly reaching out to all team members to become more actively involved in the organization while also encouraging team members to explore their passions.

A recent hire, for instance, showed a big interest in the field of hardscaping. Even though he didn't have a day of experience in hardscaping, the organization hired him on because of how strongly his core values aligned with the organization's, and six months later he'd driven the GreenEarth hardscaping team to be more efficient and profitable than ever.

"His attitude and beliefs fit in with ours seamlessly, and it's like he's been a member of the team since we first started," said Jeremy. "And because we put that trust in him, because we're so adamant about everyone aligning with our core values, we've had great success in that field. The Habits have helped us with everything from hiring to efficiency to really taking our business to the next level—allowing us to

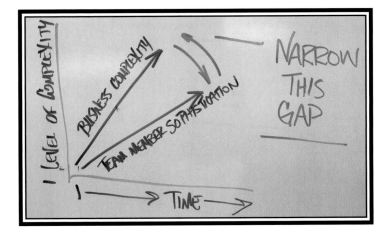

create opportunity for our employees and grow in ways that we never thought possible."

"If you'd asked me a year ago, if we could take our organization to $50 million in revenue in less than ten years, I would have said you were crazy; but now, with the insights from Petra Coach and everything they've taught and shown us, it seems like it's actually possible. If we didn't have the courage to push ourselves and our team out of our comfort zone, who knows how many years down the road we'd still be fighting the same battles. Learning to believe in ourselves, in something bigger than ourselves, has really helped open up so many opportunities that I never would have thought about," Jeremy added. "It's been a journey. And in the end, it's not what we get as people in life or in business life. It's really about who we've become." ❧

GREENEARTH LANDSCAPE SERVICES: CASE STUDY TAKEAWAYS

One of the most powerful things Jeremy learned during the first session with Petra Coach was how little of what he was trying to communicate to the team was coming through. Not only were they on different pages, it suddenly seemed like they were on completely different books.

The most resistance to the Habits was during the first round of planning sessions. But after round two, people became more excited and involved, and by round three, a lot more people were self-starting and generally becoming more excited about the process.

Implementing core values and purpose were an important turning point for the organization.

The OPPPs were difficult for several members of the team to fill out, but the process was a significant first step. It's helped many of the team members' not only in their business lives but also in their personal lives.

Huddles were also very difficult to implement, especially with two locations, but once they were able to get them going, it created an unprecedented unity between the two divisions.

In establishing a long-term goal for the organization, and identifying the steps needed to get there year-over-year, the organization now believes it will reach a goal it once thought impossible: $50 million revenue in less than ten years.

CHAPTER 10

HEALTHCARE BLUEBOOK

Cohesive Organization with a Team That Doubles in Size Each Year

BUSINESS TYPE

Healthcare cost/quality database for companies and consumers

NUMBER OF EMPLOYEES

80+

LOCATION

Nashville, TN

Healthcare Bluebook didn't have any challenges with growing their organization when they got in touch with Petra Coach. In fact, their problem was the opposite—growth that was happening so fast that it was presenting immediate challenges to organization planning and communications. They needed a system that would help them get both of these under control and built in such a way that allowed for exponential growth over the next several years.

"We'd read Rockefeller Habits as a team some time ago and had adopted some of the practices on our own, but it wasn't formalized," explained Zack Samples, SVP of analytics for Healthcare Bluebook. "As we continued to grow, we realized we really needed someone who could facilitate the implementation process, so we got in touch with the author of *Mastering the Rockefeller Habits*, Verne Harnish, and asked if there was anyone who could help walk us through this. He told us there was someone right in our backyard and introduced us to Andy and the Petra Coach team."

ABOUT HEALTHCARE BLUEBOOK

Healthcare Bluebook is an organization founded on the simple yet powerful idea of creating fairness in the healthcare marketplace.

As a physician, founder, and CEO, Dr. Jeff Rice was familiar with the doctor-side of healthcare, but when his twelve-year-old son needed foot surgery, he learned far more about the patient side than he expected.

"It was a one-hour outpatient foot surgery, and I was able to find a really good doctor who could do it," Dr. Rice explained. "But when I called the facility to ask about the price, they had no idea what it was going to be. They said they had to research it and get back with me. When they did, the price was way too high. 'Somewhere between $15,000 and $25,000,' they said. So I called the surgeon and asked if there was another facility that would be appropriate for the surgery. There was another facility that was just as good, even more convenient, and the price was just $1,500."

It was the same surgery, same surgeon, just two different facilities, three blocks apart, and with a total savings of between $13,500 and $23,500.

This was something that every patient in America had to deal with every day, all day long, Dr. Rice realized, so he set out to find a way that allowed patients throughout the country to easily navigate the healthcare system and find care that was appropriate and affordable.

BUILDING THE BOOK

Healthcare Bluebook has been employee-owned since the very beginning. At first, it was just people putting their spare time into doing the right thing for patients, slowly building up the shopping platform one block at a time.

The first product, released in 2007, was a basic public website that explained fair pricing and how to look up the local cost of various healthcare services. Before long, however, they realized that this information was something employers were interested in as well and began developing a premium option that included cost- and quality-variation analytics, procedure-specific reporting, measures of annual outcome and return on investment, and open integration with existing employer-sponsored programs, among other features.

Every year for six years after the premium option became available in 2009, the organization experienced 100 to 300 percent growth year-over-year, and even though they were following some of the Rockefeller Habits, the team realized they needed to get serious about formal organization. That's where Petra Coach came in, although several people at the organization weren't exactly over-the-top about it.

"People were very skeptical," said Mike O'Neil, partner at Healthcare Bluebook. "Most of our executive team had been at larger companies before they joined us and had been through lots of different planning processes, strategic meetings, budgeting processes, and similar endeavors, and they were pretty uniformly negative about the idea."

After the two-day session with the Petra team, however, everyone was onboard 100 percent.

"A LITTLE CLUNKY AT FIRST"

Right off the bat, Bluebook implemented the quarterly planning process and clarified their core values and purpose statement.

Just like with the executive team, the staff at Bluebook was resistant to the new structure and processes that were "a little clunky at first." Formal daily huddles, for instance, weren't implemented until about four or five months in, and getting everyone on board with daily updates was a struggle.

"Communication had been a real issue before we started the daily huddles. People didn't feel like they were 'in the know.' But once we got the daily huddles going, it became this nice, energetic way for people to start their day. It also gave them a real sense of involvement and teamwork. It's had a real impact on our culture that way," said Dr. Rice.

"Like a few other Habits we were doing pre-Petra Coach, we were doing the huddles but not effectively and not the best way we could," said Zack.

"Involving more team members in the entire process was huge," said Dr. Rice. "We had priorities before we implemented the Habits, but we didn't have a way to rally around them. So setting those, displaying them, using the software tool Align to manage them, and getting everyone excited about them has been very valuable. And since we generated the core values as a leadership team of coworkers, it felt right as a group. They were real, accurate, and reflected our culture."

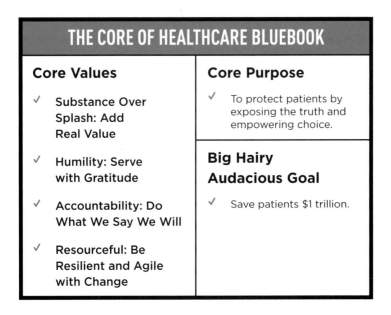

THE CORE OF HEALTHCARE BLUEBOOK	
Core Values	**Core Purpose**
✓ Substance Over Splash: Add Real Value	✓ To protect patients by exposing the truth and empowering choice.
✓ Humility: Serve with Gratitude	**Big Hairy Audacious Goal**
✓ Accountability: Do What We Say We Will	✓ Save patients $1 trillion.
✓ Resourceful: Be Resilient and Agile with Change	

The quarterly themes were another part of the Habits that Bluebook implemented after that first planning session, and each one has been well received and has provided a way for everyone in the organization to rally around priorities.

For now, quarterly themes at the organization revolve around the core values with the first theme, "Moving on Up," and reflecting Bluebook's "resourceful" value as the organization moved buildings.

Another theme, "30 for 30," aimed at collecting thirty patient-success stories and thirty core-value stories from team members, and the "Saved by the Bell" theme focused on internal education and training on Bluebook and processes.

If you'd visited the Bluebook offices during this last theme, you'd have had no doubt as to the organization's quarterly theme: a fifteen-foot-long blackboard was set up along the front entrance wall with construction paper rectangles spelling out "Saved by the Bell."

On the board was the homework: "Take courses and learn about Bluebook. Each course = 5 points. A+ = 30 points." Below that were opportunities for extra credit and across the rest of the board were dates, times, and topics for classes over the next two months.

Team members were clearly on board with the extra credit, which included "recognize a coworker exhibiting core values." Across the entire bottom length of the blackboard were cards that read, "Living the Values," featuring handwritten recognitions from one coworker to another. Midway through the theme, there was no room left to squeeze another recognition—additional cards were being taped to the wall where they'd fit.

WHAT OUR MEMBERS ARE SAYING

"The rhythm of daily, weekly, monthly, quarterly meetings has been the secret sauce to making sure that I, personally, am working on the business instead of in the business."

"People are really getting behind these," said Dr. Rice. "That's honestly the one thing I was surprised about. I really was. I was surprised at the level of effort people put into the quarterly themes. And having quarterly deadlines on things we think are important has also helped quite a bit."

THE RIGHT FRAMING UP FOR SCALING UP

For an organization growing at a breakneck pace, formal organization and efficiency in process are vital. And as Bluebook continues to put the hard work and time into ingraining the Habits into their culture, they've begun to reap the benefits of their efforts.

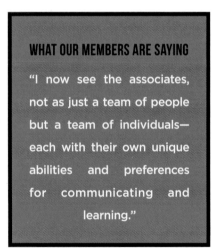

WHAT OUR MEMBERS ARE SAYING

"I now see the associates, not as just a team of people but a team of individuals—each with their own unique abilities and preferences for communicating and learning."

"Individually, we definitely all feel the impact on the efficiency front," said Dr. Rice.

"The efficiency has absolutely improved," said Zack. "We're not just jumping in to solve another person's problem; we're giving them the support and guardrails and metrics they need to run with it and then supporting them when they need it instead of trying to do it ourselves. In the past, meetings with team members created additional work for me. Now, when we end a meeting, they have full ownership and accountability for the tasks and priorities discussed."

"The DiSC profiling that Petra's team helped us with has also been beneficial," said Mike. "It allowed us to just be open and honest about how we work as individuals and how to better work as a team. If a certain job requires this kind of approach over another, then we're clear going into it on what to expect from the people involved. We don't expect them to 'change their spots,' so to speak."

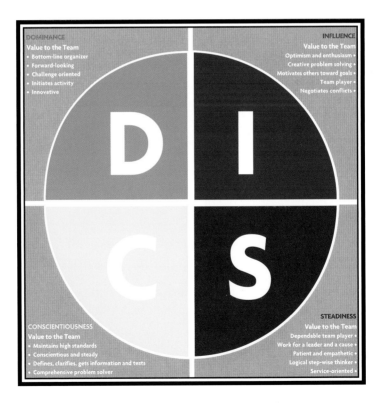

"On the whole, implementing the Habits has really helped us with the framing up of our organization for scaling appropriately," Mike added. "Part of that is making sure we're clear about the delegation and authority and things like that, but ultimately it's about accountability. You can't really delegate very well if you don't have line-of-sight to what's actually happening."

"I'd echo Mike and Zack," Dr. Rice agreed, "and just having insight into what everyone else is doing allows me to better coordinate and coach and facilitate and support all the folks on my team. So for me, personally, the Rockefeller Habits have given me a new and improved appreciation on clarity and accountability on the things we say we're going to do. We need to be clear about what those things are and what success means and then have the ability to track that so it's clear whether we got them accomplished or not. That's enormous."

"Even though we've accomplished a lot, I still feel like we're very early on in this organization," Dr. Rice added. "I still think there's a whole lot left for us to learn, and I don't think I've stopped understanding how we can improve."

"If you're in a high-growth organization, you have to get ahead of the curve. The sooner you start, the better. For two-plus years we tried to get the Rockefeller Habits going on our own and we never even came close to the progress we've made in the past year and a half." ❧

HEALTHCARE BLUEBOOK: CASE STUDY TAKEAWAYS

The leadership team was onboard with implementing the Rockefeller Habits but needed someone to facilitate the implementation process. Every year, the organization has experienced 100 to 300 percent growth, which drove the realization of the need for formal organization.

Involving more team members in the planning process was a powerful step and has proven to be incredibly valuable. Efficiency has also improved across the board, and all team members have felt the impact.

Align has given us visibility across our fast-moving organization and aided us tremulously in speeding up decision making.

Quarterly themes have been well received and are helping to drive team member involvement on all levels.

The use of DiSC profiling has also been beneficial and improved team members' ability to be open and honest about how they work together. People now accept that they shouldn't expect others to "change their spots."

The Habits have helped HCBB frame their organization for scaling up and improved line-of-sight into what's actually happening in the organization by emphasizing the importance of accountability.

CHAPTER 11

LITWINIUK & COMPANY

Creating the Ideal Workplace

BUSINESS TYPE:

Family-owned law firm / barrister and solicitors

NUMBER OF EMPLOYEES:

40+

LOCATION:

Calgary, Alberta, Canada

B egun as a single-person law practice in 1976, Litwiniuk & Company has grown as many small businesses do over the years—organically.

"You bolt a piece on here and you add a person there and you do a little something different over there and it just continues to build on the original structure," said lawyer Fred Litwiniuk, director of business development and marketing. "That's not to say that my parents didn't think about where they wanted to go with the company, but when you have the kind of growth we've had, you're just doing what you can to keep up with it."

By the late 2000s, growth at Litwiniuk had finally gotten to the point where the family had to sit down for a serious talk about the future. Both of founder Larry Litwiniuk's sons, Fred and Todd, had joined the firm—Todd as a practicing attorney and Fred as director of business development and marketing—and both were concerned not only about managing their company's growth but also about helping their parents plan for retirement.

"We brought in a consultant who worked with us, prior to working with Petra Coach, on structure and helped us develop a succession plan," said Fred. "It was a good learning experience for us, but the main thing we got out of it was the understanding that a consultant wasn't going to solve our problems. We were going to have to do the work ourselves if we were going to make this happen."

Around that same time, Fred's brother and managing partner for Litwiniuk & Company, Todd Litwiniuk, joined the Entrepreneurs' Organization (EO) and after his first few meetings, he brought home copies of *Mastering the Rockefeller Habits* for everyone to read.

"We enjoyed the book and ended up attending an EO Key Executive Program event at MIT where Andy was serving as a moderator," said Fred. "At that point we were familiar with the Rockefeller Habits and were able to see a little bit of Andy's process and meet with entrepreneurs who were making the Habits happen."

Fred and Todd went away from the event excited about implementing the Habits. The company had grown to about thirty people, and it wasn't possible for both of them to be everywhere at once. They knew that they needed to set some ground rules and share their vision of the company and what they were trying to accomplish with the whole organization.

"We just felt that implementing the Rockefeller Habits was a very attractive way to do that," said Fred.

"The survey invites honest feedback," said Fred. "We knew that there were some underlying issues—it was one of the reasons for putting this structure in place—but when they suddenly came to light during the planning session, our normally reserved group started to get into it a little bit. And that was good, but Petra Coach's team certainly earned their keep with us that day."

Even before the first coaching sessions took place, Fred and Todd were already tackling the issues of building trust in the company and getting away from the false perception of harmony.

"We wanted to encourage some honest discussion and some conflict," said Fred. "We knew that was the only way we were going to get better. A year and a half later, Petra Coach still struggles somewhat to get our team to be a little more boisterous and animated, but that's not only a function of our culture but also our profession. People in the legal industry tend to be more reserved, but we've certainly loosened up."

A year later, when the staff at Litwiniuk & Company took the anonymous survey again, the results were almost polar opposites—and it was all positive.

"If you compare the survey results from our first year with those from a year later, it's absolutely night and day," said Fred. "In one year's time, a lot of those underlying negative emotions had disappeared. That doesn't mean that we don't still have conflict or that we don't have things we need to work on or talk about, but in terms of improvement and the feel of the team, there's been a huge improvement year over year."

After addressing the survey results, the second order of business was to begin work on the foundational elements of the Habits, starting with the core values.

GETTING TO THE CORE

"It was a big thing for us, going through the discovery of our core values and really understanding what the foundational elements of our company were going to be," said Fred. "We knew that these values were going to be essential to our company's structure. They were the things we'd hire and fire for, that we'd live and die by. It was a great place to get started."

THE CORE OF LITWINIUK & COMPANY

Core Values

✓ Own It—YOU Make a Difference.

✓ Empathy—Walk the mile AND take the extra step.

✓ Kindness—Help others feel GREAT about themselves.

✓ Ask Why—Bring new ideas, CHALLENGE the status quo.

✓ Don't Blame— Point the finger at YOURSELF first.

Core Purpose

✓ We balance the power.

Big Hairy Audacious Goal

✓ To be Canada's preferred provider of consumer legal services.

Once the team had the values down on paper, the next step was bringing them to life. How to go about this was one of the main points of discussion during the rest of that first group session, and it's still something that Litwiniuk & Company focuses on regularly today.

"The number-one game changer for our business was forming and implementing those core values," said Fred. "I can't overstate that. We use our core values as a way to help others in the organization understand from a broad perspective what it is we're achieving in our workplace. They're the blueprint for making decisions and determining how you're going to treat your colleagues as well as your clients."

"REGULAR MEETINGS REPLACE DISTRACTIONS"

The meeting rhythm has been one of the most beneficial aspects of the Habits for Litwiniuk and not just because it provides a clear framework for fostering the deeper attributes of the Habits but because it allows for an open collaboration and dispersion of thoughts on how to solve various legal issues.

"The lawyers at our office are very collaborative, which is a wonderful thing," Fred explained. "They love to bounce ideas off of one another and talk about how to solve specific legal issues. That's great, but when you've got a dozen lawyers, our thought was that it would be much better if they had that conversation in front of the group so that everyone could benefit from that learning."

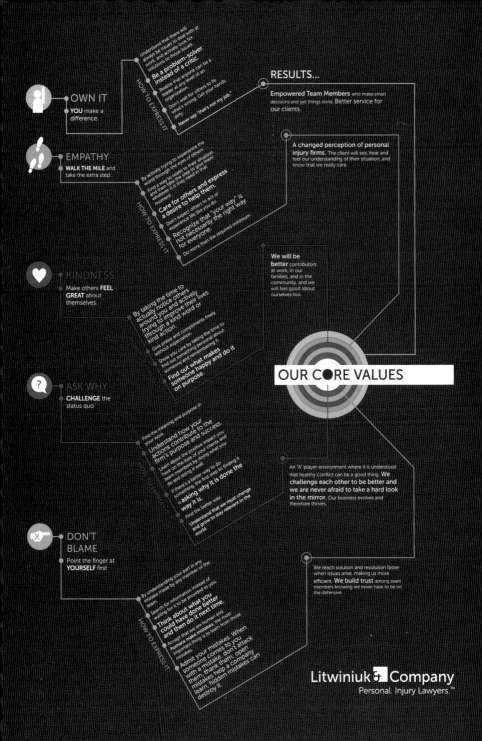

OWN IT
YOU make a difference.

EMPATHY
WALK THE MILE and take the extra step.

KINDNESS
Make others FEEL GREAT about themselves.

ASK WHY
CHALLENGE the status quo

DON'T BLAME
Point the finger at YOURSELF first

HOW TO EXPRESS IT

Understand that there will always be issues to deal with at work, and actively look for solutions to those issues.
Be a problem-solver instead of a critic
Realize that anyone can be a leader at any level of an organization.
Don't wait for others to fix what's wrong. Get your hands dirty.
Never say "that's not my job."

By actively trying to experience the world through the eyes of others
Find a way to relate to their situation and then take the step to give them whatever it is they need in that moment.
Care for others and express a desire to help them.
Don't expect others to act or experience life like you do.
Recognize that your way is not necessarily the right way for everyone.
Do more than the required minimum.

By taking the time to actually notice others around you and actively trying to improve their lives through a kind word or kind action.
Give praise and compliments freely without expectation.
Show you care by taking the time to find out something personal about someone and remembering it.
Find out what makes someone happy and do it on purpose.

Find the meaning and purpose in your work.
Understand how your actions contribute to the firm's purpose and success.
Learn about the positive impact you have on the lives of your clients and team members by doing what you do and doing it well.
If there's a better way to do something, the first step to finding it is asking why it is done the way it is.
Find the better way.
Understand that we must change and grow to stay relevant in the world.

By understanding your part in any mistake made by any member of the team.
Search for information instead of waiting for it to be provided to you.
Think about what you could have done better and then do it next time.
Accept that we are human and humans make mistakes, the most important thing is to learn from those mistakes.
Admit your mistakes. When someone comes to you with a mistake, don't attack them, thank them; open mistakes help a company learn, hidden mistakes can destroy it.

RESULTS...

Empowered Team Members who make smart decisions and get things done. Better service for our clients.

A changed perception of personal injury firms. The client will see, hear and feel our understanding of their situation, and know that we really care.

We will be better contributors at work, in our families, and in the community, and we will feel good about ourselves too.

OUR CORE VALUES

An "A" player environment where it is understood that healthy conflict can be a good thing. We challenge each other to be better and we are never afraid to take a hard look in the mirror. Our business evolves and therefore thrives.

We reach solution and resolution faster when issues arise, making us more efficient. We build trust among team members knowing we never have to be on the defensive.

Litwiniuk & Company
Personal. Injury Lawyers.™

Litwiniuk's core value grid showing each core value, what each means, how to express each, and what the result is when expressed. This is visually designed to match their culture.

If an attorney were to go into another attorney's office with a question, for instance, the answer would disappear into the ether if no one talked about it or wrote it down. Instead, the Litwiniuks reasoned that saving that same question for the lawyer huddle would not only help the other attorneys learn, but it would benefit the firm's junior associates and even their students-at-law who were still working to become qualified lawyers. Additionally, the information shared at the huddle could be codified into a manual or FAQ that members of the firm could reference going forward.

"Eventually we want to have something my brother has dubbed as 'Litwiniuk University'," Fred explained. "We have questions that are asked over and over again, so why not gather as much of our learning and understanding as possible in one place and give people a place to go and look it up?"

The meetings have also helped with intra-office communication. Whereas most team members get dozens if not hundreds of emails a day, the Litwiniuk team has found it more effective and efficient to wait for the morning huddle every day to make an announcement, which guarantees everyone is going to hear it.

"Ultimately the number of meetings and frequency of meetings are meant to take the place of some other informal interactions, reducing distractions and increasing communications, all of which are issues that people complained about on that first survey," said Fred.

"The Habits are a big-picture thing," Fred added. "When you look at a company that's running well, that's implemented the Habits, you can say, 'Well, that's running really well and that's happening well,' but when you dig in on the ground level, it's more about the basic, 'Here's when we're going to have a meeting and this is what we're going to talk about and here's who's going to meet and here's how often we should be doing this.' So it's sort of a collection of behaviors, which, taken together, lead to much more than the sum of their parts."

LIVING THE HABITS

Efficiency and collaboration have both improved greatly for Litwiniuk & Company since implementing the Habits.

"I find more and more now that people in the company are much more willing to get out there and find a solution instead of waiting for someone to fix something, which was how it was before the Habits," said Fred. "As time goes on, things get taken care of, things happen, and people are taking initiatives and driving the company forward without necessarily having to be explicitly told that something needs to be done."

Having worked with consultants, the Litwiniuks knew that there was fundamental work that needed to be done in their organization that couldn't be done by a consultant. They needed to be coached on how to approach it, and then they needed to do it for themselves.

"The coaching model has been amazing for us," said Fred. "It's really shown us that we're capable of achieving more than we thought we could, that we could have a better team than we thought possible, and that we could achieve the kinds of success that maybe we weren't convinced that we could."

"Todd and I wanted this place to be more deliberate in its design than our parents did, but then again, they didn't have that luxury," Fred added. "We were standing on the shoulders of giants and we had the luxury to think about those things, so we did. We sat down and said, 'What kind of place do we want to come to work at every day?' We wanted a place where people were happy, they were engaged, and they enjoyed working with one another. We've been deliberate about creating that and we've been able to make this place into what we wanted it to be." ❖

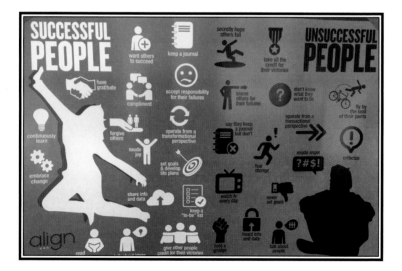

LITWINIUK & COMPANY: CASE STUDY TAKEAWAYS

From the very beginning of their work with Petra Coach, one of the hardest things for the firm to learn was to be comfortable with a certain level of uncertainty.

It was also difficult for the team to address the results of the anonymous survey conducted before the first planning session. The leadership team was aware that it had underlying issues, but having those come to light during the planning session resulted in the ignition of their typically reserved group. It was good, but it was an emotionally draining experience. A year later, the anonymous survey results were almost a polar opposite to the results of the first survey—and it was all positive.

Establishing meeting rhythms has also provided a clear framework for the Habits and allows for open collaboration and dispersion of thoughts between team members. Huddles have also improved intra-office communications, cutting down on the number of distracting, informal interactions.

Implementing the Habits has improved both efficiency and collaboration for the law firm. Team members are also more willing to seek out a solution instead of waiting for someone else to fix it. The coaching model has helped Litwiniuk build a better team and realize that it could achieve the kinds of success that they formerly didn't completely believe that they could.

CHAPTER 12

DSI

Organizational Cohesion and the Launch of a New Business

BUSINESS TYPE

Advanced litigation support, e-discovery, and digital forensics services

NUMBER OF EMPLOYEES

80+

LOCATION

Nashville, TN

D Si, an advanced litigation support and forensics services organization in Nashville, was growing rapidly—from two people to forty in an incredibly short amount of time. But cofounders Tom Turner and Kevin Tyner were increasingly cognizant of the immediate and long-term challenges this growth presented—from both personnel and operations standpoints.

"We all had our oars in the water and everyone was busy working and paddling, but we were all paddling in different directions," said Tom. "There was no alignment. People would look at our organization and say what a great business we had, growing at 20, 30-plus percent a year, but inside, we were incredibly frustrated. As our business grew it was forming cracks, and those cracks were becoming earthquakes."

For Tom, the turning point came when he began doubling down on attending Entrepreneurs' Organization (EO) meetings and realized that he was hearing the same things over and over.

"There was this repetitive messaging around culture, around processes, around people, around having core values and a core purpose, and all of a sudden, it started to make sense," said Tom. "I learned about the Rockefeller Habits when Verne came to Nashville, and I remember sitting down at the table and drinking from the fire hydrant. It was fantastic; it was how we needed to do our business.

"But then, when I started getting it going, I was overwhelmed. So I continued to work *in* my business instead of *on* my business, and it wasn't until several years later that I met with Andy."

Tom and I knew each other through EO during my NationLink days and we reconnected shortly after I'd started Petra Coach. When I told Tom what I was doing, Tom explained the problems they were having at DSi. In a nutshell, I explained that his challenge was that his revenues were growing at 20, 30-plus percent each year, but his people and processes weren't. Tom agreed and also pointed out that if he was going to implement the Rockefeller Habits, as he'd planned to so many years ago, now was the time.

The DSi team had a few Habits in place already. There were daily huddles, though they only happened three times a week and instead of fifteen minutes, they tended to run closer to forty. There was no agenda, no real tracking system, just a circle of people standing around talking about what they were working on.

"We had people whose roles and responsibilities had shifted, changed, and grown, but we didn't have adequate methods for communication, standardization, or alignment within the organization," said John Burchfield, president of

DSi. "And all that was creating friction, particularly inter-departmentally. It was a culture by default, not design. Culture begins with alignment—with accountability—and if you don't have that internally—if you're not making client deliverable deadlines and there's a fundamental lack of trust between teams—then you're in trouble."

It wasn't going to be an easy or quick process, and even before their first official planning session, the Petra Coach team made it clear that this was going to be a two- or three-year process to really get all the Habits implemented.

"I thought it was going to take three to six months," said John, smiling. "Turned out that they were right and I was wrong. It takes a while, particularly if you've got a fast-paced organization."

Another challenge was that DSi wasn't exactly a spring chicken. They'd been in business for more than a decade and old habits are notoriously hard to break.

"One of my biggest concerns at the beginning was that we were already a twelve-year-old organization and had so many bad habits," said Tom. "How were we going to get everyone to come to huddle every day? Or follow a specific structure? How were we going to get every last person in our organization to remember our core values? There was no way, I thought. Never going to happen."

"I FELT LIKE A PUNCHING BAG"

"Implementing the Habits would have been a lot easier when Kevin and I were smaller," said Tom. "Everyone kind of knew who we were, where we wanted to go, and what we stood for back then. Transparency wasn't an issue. But then we went through this doubling, over and over again, of employees until there were people working with us who I didn't even know and who didn't know me—and they definitely didn't know what we stood for."

Despite the challenges, however, Tom, Kevin, and John started pushing out the Habits in a more consistent manner, starting with explaining the organization's core values, core purposes, and the systems and processes that they were going to start putting into place.

There were mixed reviews from the start. Some people just philosophically didn't agree with it, while others thought that the leadership team would play around with this system for a few months and then give up.

"You're always going to have your holdouts and your folks who want to hang on to the way things were done previously, and there will be a skeptical period of time where you have to demonstrate the value and prove you're consistent with following through," said John. "Like any new initiative within an organization, there's going to be a decent portion of the employee base that's going to think that this new system is just the flavor of the month."

Regardless of the general attitude at the beginning, DSi's leadership team stuck with it and relentlessly hammered home the Habits.

"Every single day, we continued with the daily huddle and we continued the quarterly meetings, no matter how painful they were and how much negative feedback we got," said Tom. "It literally felt like I was a punching bag in some of those meetings, and there were days when I just wanted to throw in the towel and say 'It's not worth it; I'm doing everything I can to make this the best place possible, and people just don't get it.'"

It didn't take long for Tom, Kevin, and John to realize just how much strength and courage it takes to change a system, especially one that's been in place for so long. But as Tom pointed out, it's the same thing with fitness. Bodily change doesn't happen overnight, and when it does happen, it has to be maintained. It's the same with the internal workings of an organization.

"There's some pain, but the people who stuck with it have seen us become so much better as an organization. They endure the pain along with us because they know that it ultimately stands to benefit all of us," said Tom.

"Two years ago, we set goals for the next twelve months, thirty-six months, and sixty months," said Tom, "and I remember thinking that those goals were never going to happen. But they did. We put it out there and it happened."

PUTTING THE DSI SPIN ON THE HUDDLE

Although the core of the Rockefeller Habits remains constant no matter what business they're implemented in, companies typically adjust certain aspects of the Habits so that they fit in their construct.

For DSi, this meant switching up the daily huddles.

On Mondays, the entire organization gets together for a forty-minute meeting called AHOD, or All Hands on Deck. The team celebrates wins and victories, and each director and manager gives a report on certain KPIs. For sales, this might be an update on the pipeline, and for IT, this might be a report on the number of tickets open and closed. Any hiccups that might have happened are discussed as well as how they were worked through.

Then, on Tuesdays, Wednesdays, and Thursdays, the organization holds "rhythm huddles," in which the organization gets together to go through the Rockefeller Habits, such as: "What's the number-one most important thing I will complete today?" and "Where am I stuck?" Departments take turns giving their KPI reports on these days, with two reporting each day to keep the process moving.

Finally, Fridays are for winding down, getting to know one another, and enjoying an ice cream social. Once a month the office provides lunch to everyone, and once a quarter, Friday becomes Celebration Friday and includes several culture-boosting activities.

GETTING ALIGNED

The Align software has also become a necessary part of DSi, facilitating the huddles by allowing everyone in the organization to use the centralized web-based platform to load information, create visibility, check on priorities, and collect huddle information.

"It just gives light to the process," said John. "Tracking all of this with pen and paper and Excel spreadsheets would have been a nightmare, so for us, the whole process is intrinsic."

The software is also more in line with a generation used to consuming and accessing information digitally.

"For our team, it is just very natural to log into Align on their phones, walk into the huddle, and have their Align up and priorities up on their phones versus bringing a sheet of paper and pen and writing it all down in some way," John explained.

The only real barrier to Align, he noted, is the obverse when it comes to the digital age. So much information is kept in tracking systems that adding one more place to put information can become cumbersome.

"If I'm a salesperson, for example, I'm entering a lot of information in Salesforce and putting dates on my Outlook calendar, so having one more place to add information, especially if it's duplicate information, is hard to keep up with," said John.

"On the other hand, however, the more you use a system, the more it develops gravity. Once we had enough information in Align and enough reason to go there, then people began to use it more and more. We've got our huddle updates in there, our core values, all the supporting core documentation, the seven strata—it's all in there and because of that, the software has really become a part of our process."

NUMBER-ONE HABIT: ONE-ON-ONES

"One of the most difficult Habits to implement, but also the most rewarding, has been the one-on-one meetings every two weeks," said John. "You can get it on the schedule and have all the intent in the world to make it happen, but if someone isn't on top of those meetings, inspecting them and insisting that they take place, then other priorities might intervene and the one-on-ones get pushed to the side."

For John, the one-on-one with a manager is the linchpin for making the whole Rockefeller Habits process work.

"You can go through and set goals and have alignment for those goals, but if there's no regular check-in occurring to talk about how those priorities are progressing, where they're at on KPIs, who's helping them with their stucks, then the process falls apart," said John. "It's a domino effect. If you haven't done your one-on-one and you're not keeping up with your priorities, then your huddle updates suffer and you start wanting to skip huddle because you either don't have anything to talk about or you're behind.

"Time after time, employee engagement studies have shown that the number-one driver of employee engagement is a direct relationship and communication with the supervisor. One-on-ones may be the toughest to be consistent with, but they're also the most important."

Overall, John added, structure is something that all of us innately crave, from the most consistent and staid personalities to the most avant-garde creative.

"With busy, growing companies, it's easy to allow for not enough structure," said John. "What we needed was a platform with just the right amount of structure, and we found it. We still have pockets for freedom and creativity, but we also have that structure that's critical for any organization."

And at the heart of that structure is culture. As equally valuable as solid systems and structures, the culture at DSi is what provides its employees with a sense of engagement and connects them to the core values and core purpose that they all work toward every day.

It's such an important factor, in fact, that DSi has its very own *culture warrior*.

BRING ON THE CULTURE WARRIOR!

Justin Moses, DSi's culture warrior, actually began with the organization in sales. However, as he began attending quarterly planning sessions, he found himself volunteering to take on multiple initiatives that highlighted culture, education, and individual growth.

"One of the first responsibilities I took on was our first quarterly theme, the DSi University, and ran with it," said Justin. "That was four years ago, and since then it's grown to the point where we have a full learning-management software dedicated to it, with more than two hundred individual lessons for training individuals in our organization."

Meanwhile, it had become obvious to the leadership team that Justin wasn't as excited about sales as he was about the culture initiatives he was driving for the organization.

"I explained that I saw a need for a cultural position to take on DSi University, the quarterly themes, and employee growth. I felt that was where my assets were and that I could contribute to the organization that way, and luckily, they agreed," said Justin.

Thanks to Justin's efforts, DSi now not only has a thriving DSi University but a top-notch community-outreach program called DSicover Your Community and an employee-development program called DSicover You, which focuses on employees living out the organization's core values and purpose.

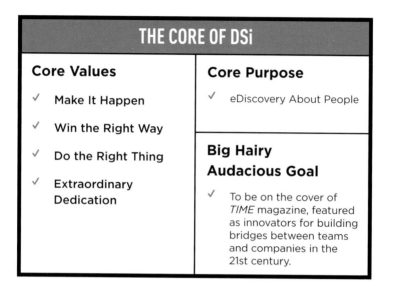

THE CORE OF DSi	
Core Values	**Core Purpose**
✓ Make It Happen	✓ eDiscovery About People
✓ Win the Right Way	
✓ Do the Right Thing	**Big Hairy Audacious Goal**
✓ Extraordinary Dedication	✓ To be on the cover of *TIME* magazine, featured as innovators for building bridges between teams and companies in the 21st century.

Quarterly themes have also been a strong focus for Justin, with programs such as Huddle Heroes and Communication Olympics.

With Huddle Heroes, team members were encouraged to increase their use of the Align software and participate in huddles. Teams gained points the more they participated in both and, depending on their score, were either dubbed "superheroes" or "villains." At the apex of the leaderboard was Spider-Man and at the bottom was the Green Goblin. Then, each week during Monday's All Hands on Deck, the Spider-Man team got to spritz the Green Goblin team with "web fluid" (a.k.a. Silly String).

Communication Olympics, on the other hand, was created around feedback gathered from the quarterly planning sessions. Survey results pointed toward frustrations in communication. DSi leadership took that feedback and faced it head on.

Corresponding with the 2016 Summer Olympics, the organization hung national flags throughout the office and created events around communications for different teams (countries) to participate in. They held opening ceremonies during an All Hands on Deck meeting and even had an anti-doping committee for those who didn't abide by email or meeting policies. Through this theme, DSi was able to increase its communications-confidence rating and develop additional lessons in DSi U. Team Canada took the gold and was rewarded with personal massages.

Justin also has several ongoing culture initiatives underway. Apart from DSi University, there's the Applause Board, where employees recognize one another for embodying DSi's core values with handwritten notes of thanks; the DSi Hall of Fame, which is selected based on applauses on the Applause Board, with one winner for each core value each quarter and an overall winner selected each year (the winners have their caricatures drawn and displayed throughout the year and their signatures burned on the floor-to-ceiling wooden Wall of Fame); and the DSi Wheel of Destiny, which quarterly Hall of Fame nominees get to spin for unique gifts or experience-based prizes such as tickets to Sky High Sports or Escape Nashville.

The DSicover You theme is a permanent fixture in the employee break room. Spelled out in neon lights across the top of the display, DSicover You consists of a simple yet powerful system of jars and tokens. Each team member's picture is posted next to his or her mason jar with a personal goal written just below the image. Goals can be anything from "lose twenty pounds" to "quit smoking" to "run a marathon." Above each image are two large jars displaying the programs tagline, "Better You. Better Us." The Better You jar contains tokens representing the potential and accomplishments of individuals, and the Better Us jar contains completed tokens that represent what the team has accomplished.

As each team member creates a goal, a token value is assigned to it and the jar is filled. When the team member accomplishes that goal, all the tokens are poured in the Better Us jar and the team member gets to ring an old-fashioned boxing bell, signifying the end of the fight.

When the Better Us jar reaches a designated number of tokens, the entire organization is rewarded with a fun experience and a vacation package for two is raffled off to those who contributed to the jar.

"Culture is interesting, especially in our industry because we're dealing with attorneys and multi-million-dollar cases," said Justin. "We have client-services team members who may be working until two or three in the morning, and while they may see some of the culture programs we're doing, they may not have time for them. Everyone doesn't participate every time, but when they do, I feel like it hits them at the right time, when they truly need it.

"Having these culture programs, like Hall of Fame and DSicover You, brings everyone together for something other than work. Just getting to know people other than just what they do at work helps you understand those you work with on a more personal level and helps you work with them better.

"It can be difficult to get people to participate, but it's that much more rewarding when they do. And it's contagious! It's enriching lives while also increasing our retention rate and luring top talent to our team."

STAYING IN THE HABIT

For the entire DSi leadership team, implementing the Rockefeller Habits couldn't have happened soon enough.

"Ultimately, if we hadn't done this, we would have fallen apart as an organization," said Tom.

John agreed. "There's a certain egoic humility required for me to say that we needed help from someone on the outside, and yet as I look at the process, I don't think anything could have gone as well as this did."

In fact, DSi has recently launched a new organization and from the beginning, they ensured that all the Rockefeller Habits were a solid part of the system.

"We're getting a second bite of the apple, so to speak," said Tom with a smile. "And we've been able to take what we've learned from DSi that's been successful and implement it there. If we could do it all over again, we'd have started the Habits from the first day DSi opened its doors." ❧

DSI: CASE STUDY TAKEAWAYS

DSi's problem was a lack of alignment. The organization was growing at 20–30 percent each year, but the structure was beginning to crumble. The DSi team attempted to get the Habits going on their own but became overwhelmed. Several years later, they decided to seek out a coach.

Part of the challenge in implementing the Habits was that the organization had already existed for more than a decade, and old habits are hard to break. Launching the Habits met with mixed reviews, and some team members just philosophically didn't agree with it.

To make the daily huddles work for them, the DSi team created a huddle structure that allowed the whole organization to collaborate without taking up an inordinate amount of time in the mornings.

The Align software also helped with facilitating the huddles, allowing team members to load information to the web-platform from either their computers or phone apps, which provided more visibility across the board.

One-on-ones (two-weekers) help DSi team members keep up with priorities, which feeds into huddles, which feeds into overall participation.

Culture is also seen as equally valuable as having solid systems and structures at DSi—so much so that the organization hired its own culture warrior. DSi has launched its own DSi University, as well as a community outreach program called DSicover Your Community, and an employee development program called DSicover You, among other culture-oriented programs.

According to DSi leadership, if they hadn't implemented the Habits, the organization would have fallen apart. Today, they've improved to the point of being able to open a new organization and have already started to implement the Habits there, as well.

CONCLUSION
DO YOU NEED A COACH?

I have the highest regard for what you do each and every day. I know, firsthand, just how difficult it is to build a business, and I applaud you—the entrepreneur, the leader, the manager, the team member—for getting up every day and fighting the good fight.

Business is hard. But it doesn't have to stay that way.

There are around sixty-five working days every quarter, with five hundred-plus hours devoted to building your business. Take just two percent of that time—a short ten hours to create a real plan for the work you and your teams are doing. Then be diligently consistent in executing that plan.

Do you need a coach to do this? No, you don't. I didn't.

But you should ask yourself: why haven't I done this stuff already?

If we at Petra Coach can help you in any way, please do not hesitate to ask. Call us, email us, message us, grab our free resources on www.petracoach.com, however you want to get in touch; because we have lived your journey and are here to help you—from answering a single question to a full engagement for implementation.

You are not alone out there.

I hope this book has given you something to think about and some insight into what to do next. No Try! Only Do.

My Best Always,

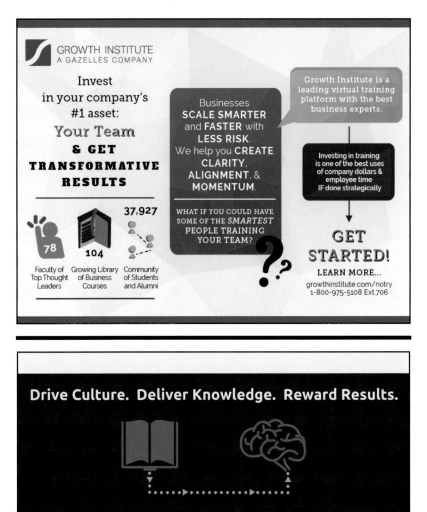

ANDY BAILEY is a serial entrepreneur who spends the majority of his time coaching other entrepreneurs, business owners, leaders, and teams to grow dynamic businesses that focus on people, strategy, execution, and cash. When he's not coaching, Andy is relaying his business and leadership experiences to readers of his recurring *Forbes*, *Huffington Post*, *SmallBizDaily*, and *AllBusiness* columns and speaking to audiences at professional events and conferences.

He is founder and head coach at Petra Coach, an entrepreneurial coaching firm. Based on his years of entrepreneurism (he started his first company in college and achieved Inc. 500 status as one of the fastest-growing businesses in America) and facilitating company-planning sessions around the globe, Andy can cut through organizational BS faster than a hot knife though warm butter.

Andy's tough love, no-BS approach combined with his real-world business experience is sure to inspire you to identify, set, and reach your wildest professional and personal ambitions.

NOTES AND TAKEAWAYS

NOTES AND TAKEAWAYS

NOTES AND TAKEAWAYS

NOTES AND TAKEAWAYS

NOTES AND TAKEAWAYS

NOTES AND TAKEAWAYS

NOTES AND TAKEAWAYS

_____

_____

_____

_____

_____

_____

_____

_____

_____

_____

_____

_____

_____

_____

_____

_____

_____

_____

_____

_____

_____

NOTES AND TAKEAWAYS

NOTES AND TAKEAWAYS

NOTES AND TAKEAWAYS

NOTES AND TAKEAWAYS

NOTES AND TAKEAWAYS